EYEWITNESS
HORSE

Kulan

Woman and girl, wearing Spanish riding costumes, on dapple gray Andalusian

Bronze statuette of warrior on horseback, c. 550 BCE

Brass rowel spur, from South America, c. 1800

Henry VIII's full horse armor

Mule drawing Indian cart, c. 1840

Bronze plaque of warrior on horseback, from Benin in modern-day Nigeria, late 16th century

Foot and two
side toes of
Anchitherium
fossil

EYEWITNESS
HORSE

Written by
Juliet Clutton-Brock

Old shoe and nails
removed from
horse's hoof

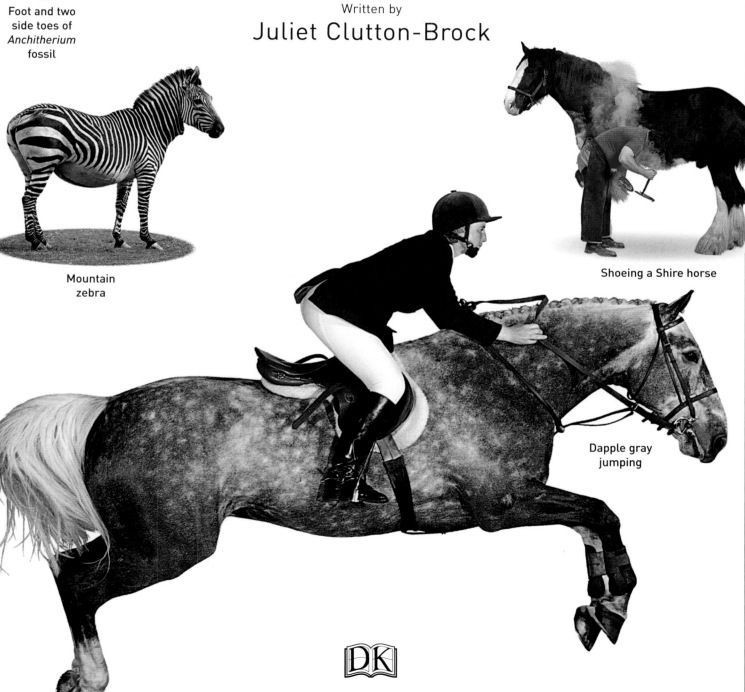

Mountain
zebra

Shoeing a Shire horse

Dapple gray
jumping

DK

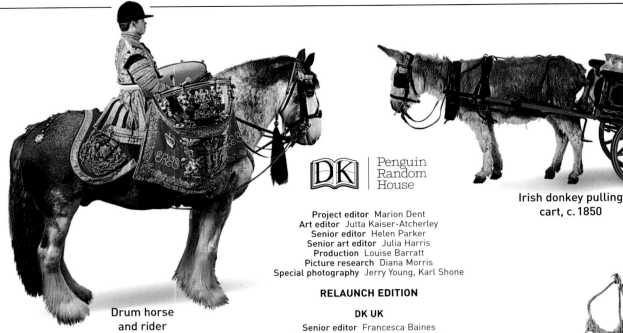

Drum horse
and rider

Irish donkey pulling
cart, c. 1850

DK | Penguin Random House

Project editor Marion Dent
Art editor Jutta Kaiser-Atcherley
Senior editor Helen Parker
Senior art editor Julia Harris
Production Louise Barratt
Picture research Diana Morris
Special photography Jerry Young, Karl Shone

RELAUNCH EDITION

DK UK

Senior editor Francesca Baines
Senior art editor Spencer Holbrook
US senior editor Margaret Parrish
Jacket coordinator Claire Gell
Jacket designer Natalie Godwin
Jacket design development manager Sophia MTT
Producer, pre-production Jacqueline Street
Producer Vivienne Yong
Managing art editor Philip Letsu
Publisher Andrew Macintyre
Associate publishing director Liz Wheeler
Design director Stuart Jackman
Publishing director Jonathan Metcalf

DK INDIA

Assistant editor Ateendriya Gupta
Art editor Alpana Aditya
DTP designer Pawan Kumar
Senior DTP designer Harish Aggarwal
Picture researcher Sakshi Saluja
Jacket designer Suhita Dharamjit
Managing jackets editor Saloni Singh
Pre-production manager Balwant Singh
Managing editor Kingshuk Ghoshal
Managing art editor Govind Mittal

Two wild
Przewalski's horses

First American Edition, 1992
This edition published in the United States in 2016 by
DK Publishing, 1450 Broadway, Suite 801, New York, NY 10018

A catalog record for this book is available from the Library of Congress.

ISBN: 978-1-4654-5174-3 (Paperback)

ISBN: 978-1-4654-5175-0 (ALB)

DK books are available at special discounts when
purchased in bulk for sales promotions, premiums,
fund-raising, or educational use. For details,
contact: DK Publishing Special Markets,
1450 Broadway, Suite 801, New York, NY 10018
SpecialSales@dk.com

Printed and bound in China

A WORLD OF IDEAS:
SEE ALL THERE IS TO KNOW

www.dk.com

Palomino with
Western-style bridle
and saddle

Archer on horseback,
c. fifth century BCE

French-style barouche, c. 1880

Pair of grays
with English
phaeton, c. 1840

Contents

Pair of Dutch Gelderlanders pulling covered waggon

The horse family

Horses, asses, and zebras belong to one family of mammals named the "Equidae." They are called "odd-toed" animals because they have only one hoof on each foot, whereas cows and deer have two hooves and are called "even-toed." The Equidae are classified in the order Perissodactyla, alongside rhinoceroses and tapirs. All members of the horse family (equids) feed on grasses and shrubs, live in family groups, and use speed to escape predators. Domestic horses vary in size but they all belong to one species—*Equus caballus*. The various parts of a horse are called the "points" of the horse.

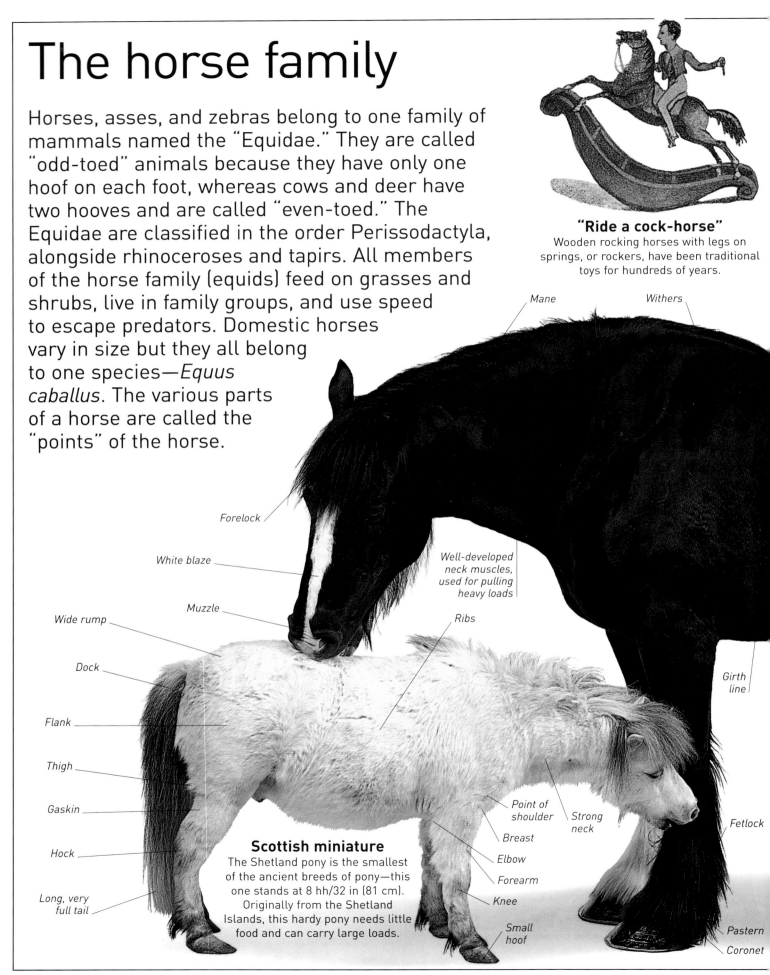

"Ride a cock-horse"
Wooden rocking horses with legs on springs, or rockers, have been traditional toys for hundreds of years.

Mane

Withers

Forelock

White blaze

Muzzle

Wide rump

Dock

Flank

Thigh

Gaskin

Hock

Long, very full tail

Well-developed neck muscles, used for pulling heavy loads

Ribs

Girth line

Point of shoulder

Strong neck

Breast

Elbow

Forearm

Knee

Small hoof

Fetlock

Pastern

Coronet

Scottish miniature
The Shetland pony is the smallest of the ancient breeds of pony—this one stands at 8 hh/32 in (81 cm). Originally from the Shetland Islands, this hardy pony needs little food and can carry large loads.

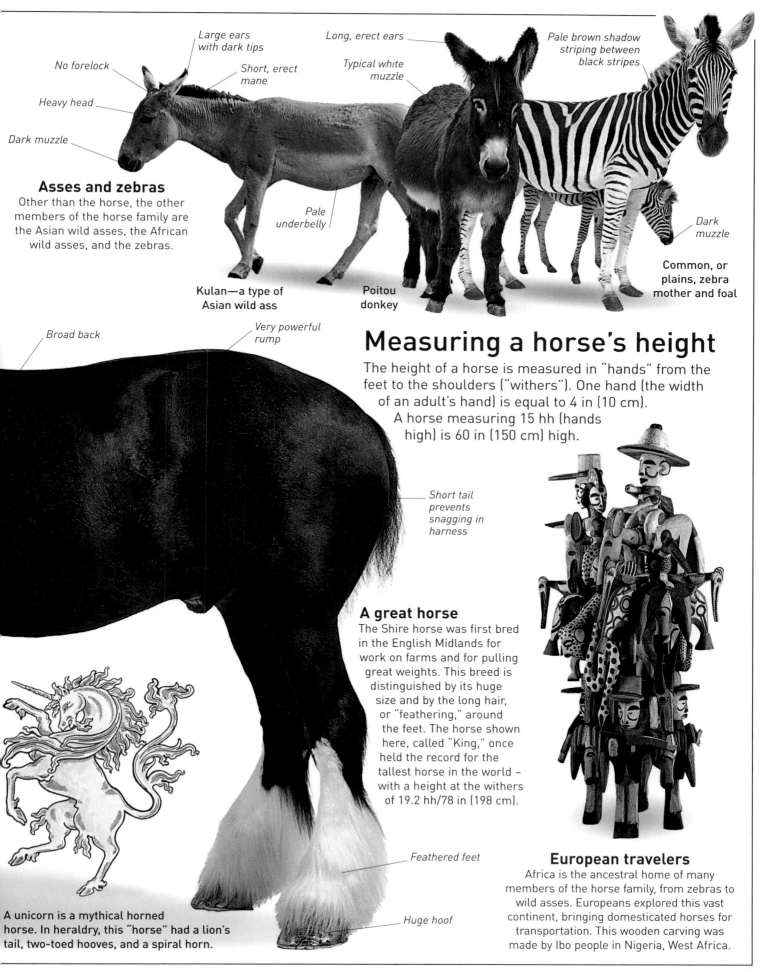

Asses and zebras

Other than the horse, the other members of the horse family are the Asian wild asses, the African wild asses, and the zebras.

No forelock

Large ears with dark tips

Heavy head

Short, erect mane

Dark muzzle

Pale underbelly

Kulan—a type of Asian wild ass

Long, erect ears

Typical white muzzle

Poitou donkey

Pale brown shadow striping between black stripes

Dark muzzle

Common, or plains, zebra mother and foal

Measuring a horse's height

The height of a horse is measured in "hands" from the feet to the shoulders ("withers"). One hand (the width of an adult's hand) is equal to 4 in (10 cm). A horse measuring 15 hh (hands high) is 60 in (150 cm) high.

Broad back

Very powerful rump

Short tail prevents snagging in harness

A great horse

The Shire horse was first bred in the English Midlands for work on farms and for pulling great weights. This breed is distinguished by its huge size and by the long hair, or "feathering," around the feet. The horse shown here, called "King," once held the record for the tallest horse in the world – with a height at the withers of 19.2 hh/78 in (198 cm).

Feathered feet

Huge hoof

A unicorn is a mythical horned horse. In heraldry, this "horse" had a lion's tail, two-toed hooves, and a spiral horn.

European travelers

Africa is the ancestral home of many members of the horse family, from zebras to wild asses. Europeans explored this vast continent, bringing domesticated horses for transportation. This wooden carving was made by Ibo people in Nigeria, West Africa.

How horses evolved

It took about 55 million years for the present family of horses, asses, and zebras (equids) to evolve from their earliest horselike ancestor. Originally called *Eohippus*, it is now known as *Hyracotherium*. In the woods of Europe, North America, and eastern Asia, this small horse was a "browsing" animal, feeding on leaves and shrubs, with four hoofed toes on its front feet and three on its hind feet. Over millions of years, it became a "grazing" (grass-eating) mammal with three hoofed toes, and later with a single hoof, on all feet. As grassland replaced woodland in North America, ancestral horses evolved longer limbs to escape predators and high-crowned teeth to chew tough grass. The first grazing horse was *Merychippus*, which was replaced by *Pliohippus*, the first one-toed horse, and later gave rise to *Equus*.

Side toe

Hoof of side toe

Main hoof-core

Side view of left hind foot of *Hipparion*

Left side toe

Right side hoof

Hoof of small side toe

Main hoof-core

Front view of hind foot of *Hipparion*

Nasal bone

Incisor tooth

Ear bone

Extinct equid

This skeleton is *Hippidion*, an extinct one-toed equid that evolved in Central America and spread to South America. Its descendant, *Onoluppidium*, survived until 12,000 years ago when human hunters moved across the continent at the end of the Ice Age.

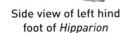

Three-toed grazer

Hipparion (side view of skull, above) was the last three-toed equid. This successful grazer had high-crowned teeth, and its fossil remains have been found in Europe, Asia, and Africa. *Hipparion* was not extinct in Africa until about 125,000 years ago.

Incisor for cutting food

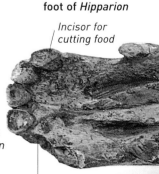

Lost incisor

Four-toed

Three-toed

Three-toed

Three-toed

One-toed

Hyracotherium

Mesohippus

Miohippus

Merychippus

Pliohippus

Browsers

Grazers

Equine sideline

The three-toed fossil horse, *Anchitherium*, spread from America through Asia and Europe about 24 million years ago. However, it was an equine sideline—one that did not evolve into the modern horse. It became extinct five million years ago.

Side toe

Side toe— hoof-core missing

Side hoof-core

Main hoof-core

Foot and toe bones of *Anchitherium*

Lower cheek teeth (molars and premolars)

Upper cheek teeth

Upper jaw of *Anchitherium*

Part of mandible (jaw bone)

Lower jaw of *Anchitherium*

The oldest equid

The palatal (roof of mouth) view of this *Hyracotherium* skull from 54 million years ago shows the square, six-lobed teeth from which modern horse teeth evolved.

Orbit, or eye socket

Palatal bone

Cranium for brain

Palatal view of *Hyracotherium* skull, showing roof of mouth

Parietal bone

Orbit

Nasal bone

Cheek teeth

Side view of right-half of *Hyracotherium* skull

High-crowned teeth used for chewing

Ear bone

Foramen magnum (hole for spinal cord)

Base of cranium

Palatal view of *Hipparion* skull

One-toed

Equus

Grazers

Three-toed first

Sheep-sized *Mesohippus* lived about 37 million years ago and was the first horse to have three toes (with the middle toe larger than the side ones).

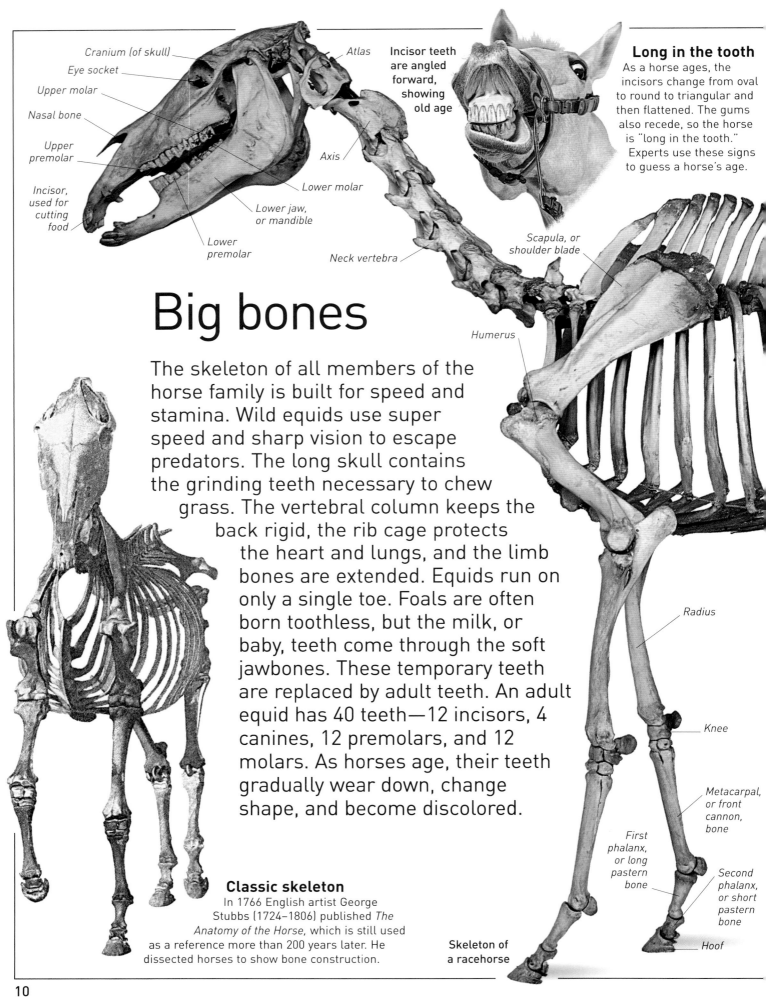

Cranium (of skull)

Eye socket

Upper molar

Nasal bone

Upper premolar

Incisor, used for cutting food

Lower premolar

Lower jaw, or mandible

Lower molar

Atlas

Axis

Neck vertebra

Incisor teeth are angled forward, showing old age

Long in the tooth
As a horse ages, the incisors change from oval to round to triangular and then flattened. The gums also recede, so the horse is "long in the tooth." Experts use these signs to guess a horse's age.

Scapula, or shoulder blade

Humerus

Radius

Knee

Metacarpal, or front cannon, bone

First phalanx, or long pastern bone

Second phalanx, or short pastern bone

Hoof

Skeleton of a racehorse

Big bones

The skeleton of all members of the horse family is built for speed and stamina. Wild equids use super speed and sharp vision to escape predators. The long skull contains the grinding teeth necessary to chew grass. The vertebral column keeps the back rigid, the rib cage protects the heart and lungs, and the limb bones are extended. Equids run on only a single toe. Foals are often born toothless, but the milk, or baby, teeth come through the soft jawbones. These temporary teeth are replaced by adult teeth. An adult equid has 40 teeth—12 incisors, 4 canines, 12 premolars, and 12 molars. As horses age, their teeth gradually wear down, change shape, and become discolored.

Classic skeleton
In 1766 English artist George Stubbs (1724–1806) published *The Anatomy of the Horse,* which is still used as a reference more than 200 years later. He dissected horses to show bone construction.

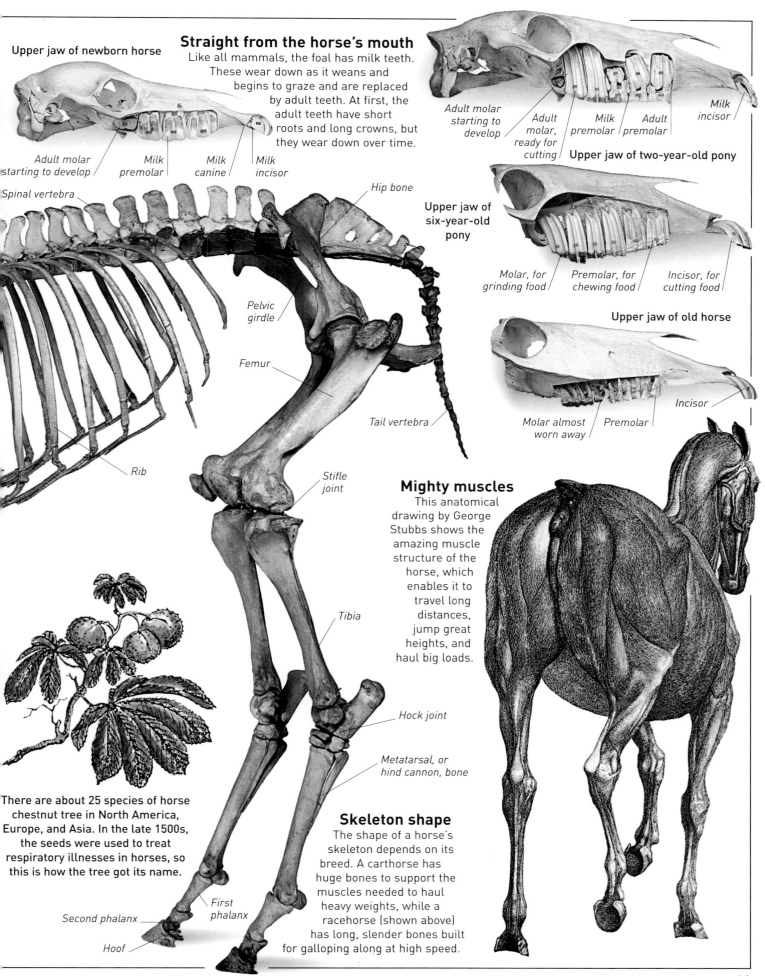

Upper jaw of newborn horse

Adult molar starting to develop / *Milk premolar* / *Milk canine* / *Milk incisor*

Straight from the horse's mouth

Like all mammals, the foal has milk teeth. These wear down as it weans and begins to graze and are replaced by adult teeth. At first, the adult teeth have short roots and long crowns, but they wear down over time.

Adult molar starting to develop / *Adult molar, ready for cutting* / *Milk premolar* / *Adult premolar* / *Milk incisor*

Upper jaw of two-year-old pony

Upper jaw of six-year-old pony

Molar, for grinding food / *Premolar, for chewing food* / *Incisor, for cutting food*

Upper jaw of old horse

Molar almost worn away / *Premolar* / *Incisor*

Spinal vertebra

Hip bone

Pelvic girdle

Femur

Tail vertebra

Rib

Stifle joint

Mighty muscles

This anatomical drawing by George Stubbs shows the amazing muscle structure of the horse, which enables it to travel long distances, jump great heights, and haul big loads.

Tibia

There are about 25 species of horse chestnut tree in North America, Europe, and Asia. In the late 1500s, the seeds were used to treat respiratory illnesses in horses, so this is how the tree got its name.

Hock joint

Metatarsal, or hind cannon, bone

Skeleton shape

The shape of a horse's skeleton depends on its breed. A carthorse has huge bones to support the muscles needed to haul heavy weights, while a racehorse (shown above) has long, slender bones built for galloping along at high speed.

Second phalanx

First phalanx

Hoof

Super senses

Horses, asses, and zebras have more highly developed senses of sight, hearing, and scent than humans. The long face of the horse is necessary not only for the large teeth, but also for the sensitive smell organs. Eyes are set high in the skull on either side of the head, so the horse has all-around vision. Ears are large, and in the asses very long, so they can point toward any sound. The horse is a herd animal, showing affection to other group members, and this loyalty is easily transferred to a human owner. This strong bond means horses will follow commands. The domestic horse and donkey retain the natural instincts and behavior patterns of their wild ancestors, such as defending their territory and suckling their foals.

Ears pointing back show submission or fear

Ears pointing forward show interest in surroundings

One ear forward, one ear back shows uncertainty

Rolling over
This pony is rolling around, as part of grooming. Rolling relaxes the muscles and helps to remove loose hair, dirt, and bugs.

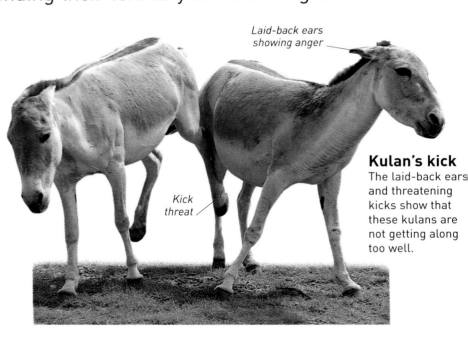

Laid-back ears showing anger

Kick threat

Kulan's kick
The laid-back ears and threatening kicks show that these kulans are not getting along too well.

Two-way stretch
An equid's ears have a dual role—to pick up sounds and transmit visual signals. If a mule (shown above) puts its ears back, it is frightened or angry. If forward, it is interested in what is happening. One ear forward and one back means it is not sure what will happen next.

Zebra calling, responding to the threat from another male

Protecting territory and family
Fighting by rearing and stabbing with the front hooves is natural to all equids. But they can also settle differences by threats with their ears, tails, and feet. Stallions fight over territory or to protect their mares, as these Icelandic ponies are doing.

Drawing shows lead horse ignoring his driver's commands and taking the liberty of stopping for a drink

Flehmen reaction
Pulling back his lips and drawing air in over his vomero-nasal organ after smelling a mare's urine, this stallion is seeing if she is ready to mate. This is the flehmen reaction.

Bite given to unfamiliar horse

A bite threat
These Przewalski's horses from two different herds are trying to show who is the more dominant, with one showing a bite threat to the other. The attacking horse's neck is thrust forward, ready to bite.

The best of friends
Two horses will often stand close together, head to tail, nuzzling each other's manes and backs, thus establishing their relationship. The frequency of these grooming and cleaning sessions varies from season to season, but they usually last about three minutes.

Ears laid back showing shock of bite attack

Mares and foals

A mare—or mother horse, ass, or zebra—gives birth to one well-developed foal after a carrying-time (gestation period) of about 11 months. The long gestation period ensures the foal is healthy enough to keep up with the herd from birth. Asses, zebras, and horses live on open grasslands where food can be scarce, and the young are an easy target for large predators. The foal stands an hour after birth and begins grazing in weeks. From one to four years, a female foal is called a "filly" and a male foal a "colt." In the wild, fillies and colts leave their mothers' herds to form new groups as they mature.

A pregnant Palomino
The large belly on this Palomino shows she will soon give birth. Pony and feral mares give birth quickly, but highly bred horses are watched in case something goes wrong.

A newborn foal
This mare is resting after giving birth to her foal, which has the birth sac over its back. Soon the foal will kick free from its mother, breaking what was the nourishing umbilical cord.

Licking into shape
The mare has gotten to her feet and removes the birth sac by licking the foal all over. This helps strengthen the foal's circulation and breathing.

Foal's erect ears showing alertness

Mother and foal
It will take almost three years for the young foal of this common zebra to become as large as its mother. The family bonds of zebras are very strong, and all the adults combine to protect their foals from any danger.

Mother nudging foal away from danger

Six-year-old common zebra mother and three-month-old foal

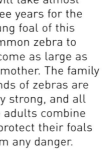

First drink
As soon as it can stand, the foal finds and sucks the mother's teats. The first milk ("colostrum") helps a foal build immunity to disease.

First steps
While the mother looks around for danger, the foal takes its first faltering steps (right).

Watch out!

This Shire mare is descended from horses that have been domesticated for thousands of years, but she still has the protective instincts of her wild ancestors.

Alert ears listening for danger

Mother's muzzle protecting foal

Height at withers 11.2 hh/ 46 in (117 cm)

Ten-year-old Shire mother and her five-week-old foal

Keeping up

A foal is on its feet within an hour of birth, and it must try to keep up with its mother—particularly in the wild.

Height at withers 17.3 hh/ 71 in (180 cm)

... And so to bed

Like all babies, a foal must rest, but it can quickly stand in case of danger.

Wild asses

There are three species of wild ass, but they are not closely related. They can interbreed, but their offspring will be infertile. The three species are the true wild ass of Africa (*Equus africanus*), which ranged over the Sahara desert in North Africa, and the two species of Asian wild asses—the onager (*Equus hemionus*) from the Middle East and northwest India, and the kiang (*Equus kiang*) from the Tibetan plateau. Of the three, the African wild ass is the ancestor of the domestic donkey. All wild asses look similar, with a heavy head, long ears, short mane, no forelock, slender legs, and a wispy tail. They are adapted for life in the semideserts and mountains of Africa and Asia. Today wild asses risk extinction from habitat loss and hunting.

Catch your onager

These scenes of catching wild onagers alive, c. 645 BCE, are from stone friezes in the palace of Nineveh in Assyria. These now-extinct Syrian onagers may have been caught for cross-breeding with domestic donkeys or horses.

Long, wispy tail

Preservation

There were several races of African wild ass until recently. The Somali wild ass (*Equus africanus somaliensis*), the only African ass in the wild, has been taken to an Israeli wildlife park to try to save the species.

Slender, pale-colored leg

Now extinct

The Nubian wild ass (*Equus africanus africanus*) is extinct. While the Somali ass has striped legs, the Nubian ass had a dark stripe across its shoulders.

Indian onagers

The Indian onager, or khur (*Equus hemionus khur*), inhabits the Thar Desert. Like all equids, khurs live in groups with an old female as herd leader. Except in mating season, adult males live in separate herds from the females.

Large ears with dark tips

No forelock

Heavy head

Dark muzzle

Short, erect, mid-brown mane

Dark stripe along back

Persian ass

The ghor-khar, or Persian onager (*Equus hemionus onager*), used to live in huge herds that migrated across the deserts in Iran, but today only a few animals survive in the wild. The onager can gallop at a speed of 30 mph (48 kph) for a long time and can jump over rocks nearly 7 ft (2 m) high.

The kulan

These onagers belong to a subspecies called the kulan (*Equus hemionus kulan*). They live in in the deserts of Turkmenistan. Kulans are 11–12 hh/44–48 in (112–122 cm) in height. In winter they grow a thick coat to protect against the icy winds. Neither the onager nor the kiang has been domesticated, although in the ancient civilizations of the Near East, onagers were probably crossed with donkeys and horses to produce strong hybrids.

Pale, almost white underbelly

Brink of extinction

The kiang (*Equus kiang*), or Tibetan wild ass, is the largest ass, at more than 14 hh/56 in (142 cm) tall. Kiangs are sacred to the Tibetans, but risk extinction from hunting and habitat loss.

Queen Puabi's rein ring features an onager in Ur's royal tombs, in ancient Mesopotamia, c. 2500 BCE.

Large, rounded ears

Seeing stripes

Today, zebras live only in Africa, but their ancestors, like all horse family members, evolved in North America. There are three living species of zebra—Grevy's, common, and mountain—in different habitats with different stripe patterns. Zebras feed on coarse grass and cross wide areas to graze. They are very social, spending time on grooming and nuzzling each other. Zebras live in family groups of 100 or more. It is not known why zebras are striped, but the pattern may make it harder for predators to single out one animal when the herd gathers together.

White ears with black tips

Big ears
The Grevy's large, round ears can signal to other zebras and listen for distant sounds.

Oval ears

Very dark muzzle

Small, squarish dewlap on throat

Thinner stripes down legs

No stripes on belly

Seven-year-old female mountain zebra

Stripes of backbone go down tail

Broad, well-marked stripes over rump

Shadows between stripes

Donkeylike tail, with hair only at its tip

Mountain zebra
The mountain zebra, *Equus zebra* (above), is today an endangered species that may soon be extinct. It is found in small numbers in the mountain ranges of the western Cape province of South Africa and up the west coast to Angola. Like the common zebra, the mountain zebra averages about 13 hh/ 52 in (132 cm) at the withers.

Six-year-old common, or plains, zebra mare and her three-month-old foal

Zebroid
Zebras can interbreed with all other horse species, but their offspring are infertile. This Zorse is a hybrid between a zebra and a horse.

Common or plains
The common zebra, *Equus burchelli*, at 13 hh/52 in (132 cm) once ranged throughout eastern and southern Africa. It is still widespread, and herds can be seen in most wildlife preserves. Young males live in bachelor groups until they form new families.

Dorsal, or back stripe, is broad and black

Very narrow stripes on face

Grevy's zebra

Grevy's zebra, *Equus grevyi*, is the northernmost species inhabiting the semidesert areas of Kenya, Ethiopia, and Somalia. It is the largest zebra, standing about 14–15 hh/56–60 in (142–152 cm), and is considered to be a relic of more primitive horse family members.

Very tall, erect mane

Rounded ears

No forelock on head

White on either side of black dorsal stripe

V-shaped, brown patch on nose

Narrow, closely spaced black stripes on a white background, especially over the withers

White underbelly

Two female Grevy's zebras, aged three to four years

Broad hooves

Stripes go down legs, ending in black coronet, next to hoof

Pale brown shadow striping between black stripes

Black dorsal stripe becomes thinner down the tail, with stripes on either side

Stripes bend around, becoming horizontal over haunches

White inside of leg with no stripes

The quagga

A fourth species of zebra, the quagga (*Equus quagga*), was found by 19th-century explorers in southern Africa. Quaggas were hunted to extinction, but attempts are now being made to recreate the species by selectively breeding plains zebras.

Zedonk

Cross-breeding between a zebra and a donkey can produce finely striped brown animals, such as these zedonks from Zimbabwe. Many zoos have successful cross-breeding programs.

Ancient ancestors

Fossil evidence reveals that at the end of the last Ice Age, 10,000 years ago, millions of horses lived wild across Europe and Asia. They belonged to one species, *Equus ferus,* that roamed in herds and made annual migrations. As grassland replaced forest, horse numbers dropped because of habitat loss and hunting until few wild horses were left. The first wild horses were tamed and domesticated in Asia and eastern Europe about 6,000 years ago, soon spreading westward. All the domestic horses in the world today are descended from these domesticated ancestors and they are classified in one species, called *Equus caballus.*

Extinct wild horse
Many 18th-century travelers to Russia saw small wild horses, called tarpan (*Equus ferus ferus*). They died out in the early 1800s. In Poland today, ponies similar to the tarpan have been bred from primitive breeds, such as the konik.

Height range at withers of 13–14 hh/ 52–56 in (132–142 cm)

Short mane

Short forelock

An ancient English pony
The Exmoor pony is an ancient breed that closely resembles the extinct tarpan, or wild pony, of eastern Europe. The ponies live in feral herds in Exmoor, England.

Light-colored muzzle, typical of wild horse

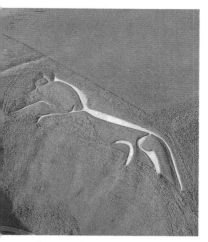

Sacred white horse
White horses were sacred to the Celts of western Europe. In about 500 BCE a horse shape was scraped into the chalk hills at Uffington in England.

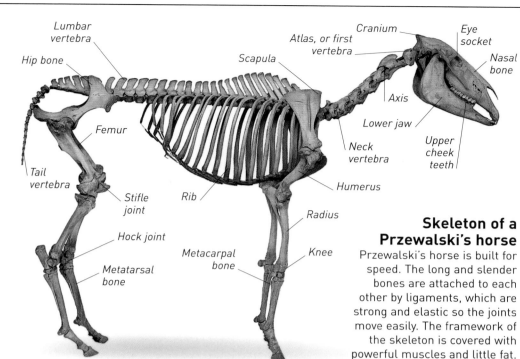

Lumbar vertebra

Hip bone

Scapula

Atlas, or first vertebra

Cranium

Eye socket

Nasal bone

Femur

Axis

Lower jaw

Neck vertebra

Upper cheek teeth

Tail vertebra

Stifle joint

Rib

Humerus

Hock joint

Radius

Metacarpal bone

Knee

Metatarsal bone

Skeleton of a Przewalski's horse
Przewalski's horse is built for speed. The long and slender bones are attached to each other by ligaments, which are strong and elastic so the joints move easily. The framework of the skeleton is covered with powerful muscles and little fat.

Przewalski's horses
Wild Przewalski's horses (*Equus ferus przewalskii*) were found in Mongolia in the 1880s, with a few bred in European zoos. They have been extinct in the wild since the 1960s, but are being reintroduced to Mongolia from herds bred in captivity.

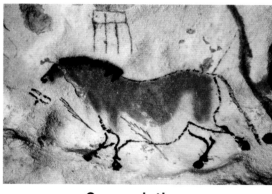

Cave paintings
This wild horse (*Equus ferus*) was painted on a wall in the famous caves at Lascaux in France by hunting people toward the end of the last Ice Age, about 14,000 years ago.

Long, shaggy tail

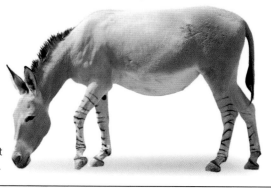

Wild African ass
The African wild ass (*Equus africanus*) is the ancestor of all domestic donkeys. It is still found in very small numbers in the eastern Sahara, but it is in danger of extinction.

Group of Przewalski's horses

Horses in history

The earliest evidence for the domestication of the horse comes from Ukraine, where people lived by herding horses and cattle on the grass steppes 6,000 years ago. At this time, the African wild ass was being domesticated in ancient Egypt and Arabia. Horses and asses were harnessed in a pair to a chariot. These chariots became a status symbol of kings, who used them for battles, parades, and hunting. By the 8th century BCE, riding horses and donkeys was a popular means of travel. The ancient Greeks and Romans built special sports arenas for chariot races.

The end of the day
This horse's head is from the Parthenon marbles (5th century BCE) in Athens, Greece. Legend goes that horses pulled the Sun's chariot to the sea each day to make the sunset, so the horse's face looks exhausted.

Royal standard
This early depiction of donkeys harnessed to a cart is on a mosaic box—the Standard of Ur—in the royal tombs of Ur in ancient Mesopotamia.

Flying through the air
In Greek mythology, Pegasus was a winged horse, springing from the blood of Medusa when Perseus, a son of Zeus, cut off her head. The horse flew to join the gods, but was caught by Athena, goddess of wisdom, and tamed with a golden bridle. This engraving of Pegasus on a bronze container was made by the Etruscans in about 300 BCE.

Half man, half horse
The myth of the centaurs—half men and half horses—may come from sightings of the horsemen of Thessaly in ancient Greece. People were unfamiliar with men on horseback, so they thought this was a new being. This scene shows the battles between the wild centaurs and the Lapiths of northern Greece.

Ready for war
This terra-cotta model from Cyprus shows an Assyrian warrior. His horse has a breastplate and headdress.

The four horses of Venice

Thought to be the work of 4th-century-BCE Greek sculptor, Lysippus, these bronze horses were taken from Constantinople (now Istanbul) in 1204 CE, to the San Marco Basilica in Venice.

Brand mark

Brands on horses have been used as proof of ownership for more than 2,000 years. This hunting scene is from a mosaic pavement (c. late 5th or 6th century BCE) discovered at Carthage, a city founded by the Phoenicians near modern-day Tunis. The mosaic was made in North Africa and shows a favorite pastime of wealthy landowners—hunting.

Surprise!

During the Trojan War of 1184 BCE, the Greeks invaded Troy by hiding soldiers inside an enormous wooden horse. The Trojans later famously wheeled the horse into the city.

A bit of a Tang

The people of China have always had a great respect for their horses. During the Tang Dynasty (618–907 CE), many earthenware models of horses were produced that are of great artistic value today. The cobalt-blue glaze was very rare and expensive to produce at that time, because cobalt was imported only in very small quantities. This figure would have been molded in several parts and then joined together as a whole.

Donkey work

The domesticated ass, or donkey (*Equus asinus*), is descended from the African wild ass (*Equus africanus*), which inhabits the hot deserts of the Sahara and Arabia. In such a harsh environment, the donkey has developed strength, stamina, and endurance to help it carry heavy loads long distances on little food and water. In the wild, donkey foals develop quickly to keep up with the herd when it travels in search of bushes and grass. Female donkeys, or jennies, carry their foals for 12 months before birth. Like all horse family members, the donkey thrives in groups.

Jesus on a donkey
When Jesus was born, the donkey was the usual transportation in Jerusalem. The "cross" on a donkey's back—a stripe down the backbone and band across the shoulders—combined with the fact that Jesus rode a donkey on the first Palm Sunday, made people believe that these hairs had healing powers.

Donkey herders
In Andalusia, Spain, donkeys are still used to help with herding and farmwork.

Greek harvest
In Greece, until recently, it was a common sight to see donkeys threshing grain. By walking around in a circle, the donkeys' hooves separate the seeds and husks.

Water, water
Water is the most precious resource in desert countries. This Tunisian woman is leading her donkey, loaded with water jars.

Rein

Breeching straps (that go around animal's haunches)

Wooden shaft

Footstand for stepping up into cart

Mid-19th-century English donkey cart

Long ears help keep donkey cool

Typical white muzzle

Lighter baby or juvenile coat on back

Darker adult coat, like his father's, now visible at first molting

Poitou donkeys

For centuries in the Poitou region of France and in Spain, there has been a tradition of breeding large donkeys to mate with female horses and produce giant mules for farmwork. Poitou donkeys stand 14 hh/56 in (142 cm) at the shoulder, or withers, making them the world's largest donkeys. They have long, shaggy coats.

Long, slender legs

White underbelly

A family group: five-year-old father, nine-year-old mother, and 11-month-old son

This poor old donkey has had a hardworking life and now deserves a peaceful retirement.

Ten-year-old Irish donkey, at 11.2 hh/46 in (117 cm)

African donkeys

These donkeys are drinking from a waterhole in Kenya where they live semi-wild on a ranch. They must fend for themselves and learn to keep away from predators.

Terret

Rein ring

Bridle

Decorated brow band

Blinker

Nose band

Bit

Collar

Trace

Girth strap

Long ears

Long tail, with tuft at tip

Trimmed hooves

Donkeys of Ireland

Donkeys are the traditional pack and haulage animals of Ireland—one of the few countries in northern Europe where they have been bred for centuries, and where they have adapted to a climate very different from the deserts in which they evolved. Irish donkeys have thicker coats and much shorter legs than donkeys from hotter regions.

Regal white donkeys

Donkeys are popular pets on farm parks. This has led to breeding for new looks, like these white donkeys. In ancient times, white donkeys were favored by royalty.

Mules and hinnies

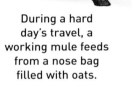

Breast collar (easier to fit than larger collar, as chest is so narrow)

Long ears like its father

During a hard day's travel, a working mule feeds from a nose bag filled with oats.

The Sumerians of Mesopotamia were the first people to interbreed horses and donkeys to produce mules (donkey father, horse mother) and hinnies (horse father, donkey mother) about 4,000 years ago. For thousands of years mules have been used as pack animals to carry huge loads, because they combine donkey stamina with horse strength. Like its parents, a mule is a herd animal that travels best in a "mule train" (a long line of mules harnessed together to pull loads). All the species in the horse family can interbreed, but the resulting offspring will be sterile.

Ancient Egyptian equids
This ancient Egyptian tomb painting from c. 1400 BCE shows a pair of horses drawing a chariot, while below two white hinnies are also pulling one. Their smaller ears show they are hinnies, not mules.

Crate of ducks

Large wheel makes it easier for donkey to pull this load

Indian travel
Mule carts have been used in Asia for 3,000 years. Early carts were attached by a wooden pole to a pair of mules, or horses. The idea of putting an animal between two wooden shafts was only invented 2,000 years ago. Above, the mule has a bridle with a bit and is driven with reins. The family's goods are piled into the cart.

14-year-old mule, 13.3 hh/55 in (140 cm), drawing Indian cart (c. 1840)

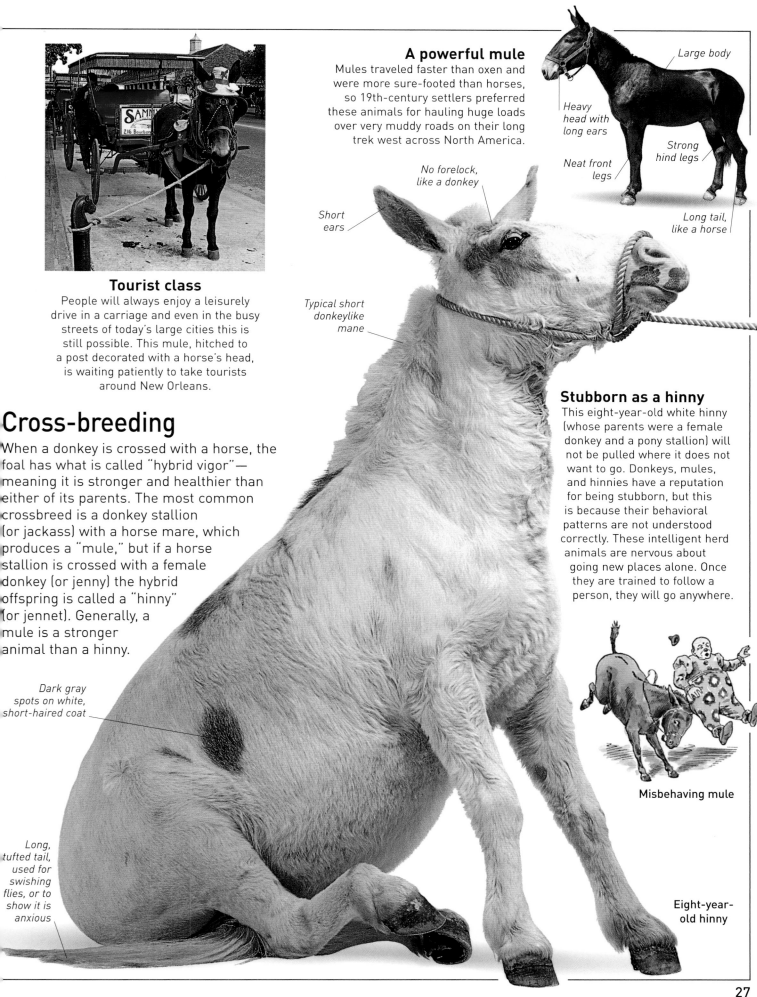

A powerful mule

Mules traveled faster than oxen and were more sure-footed than horses, so 19th-century settlers preferred these animals for hauling huge loads over very muddy roads on their long trek west across North America.

Large body

Heavy head with long ears

Neat front legs

Strong hind legs

Long tail, like a horse

Tourist class

People will always enjoy a leisurely drive in a carriage and even in the busy streets of today's large cities this is still possible. This mule, hitched to a post decorated with a horse's head, is waiting patiently to take tourists around New Orleans.

No forelock, like a donkey

Short ears

Typical short donkeylike mane

Cross-breeding

When a donkey is crossed with a horse, the foal has what is called "hybrid vigor"— meaning it is stronger and healthier than either of its parents. The most common crossbreed is a donkey stallion (or jackass) with a horse mare, which produces a "mule," but if a horse stallion is crossed with a female donkey (or jenny) the hybrid offspring is called a "hinny" (or jennet). Generally, a mule is a stronger animal than a hinny.

Dark gray spots on white, short-haired coat

Long, tufted tail, used for swishing flies, or to show it is anxious

Stubborn as a hinny

This eight-year-old white hinny (whose parents were a female donkey and a pony stallion) will not be pulled where it does not want to go. Donkeys, mules, and hinnies have a reputation for being stubborn, but this is because their behavioral patterns are not understood correctly. These intelligent herd animals are nervous about going new places alone. Once they are trained to follow a person, they will go anywhere.

Misbehaving mule

Eight-year-old hinny

New shoes

Equid hooves are made of "keratin," a protein like hair or human finger nails. Hooves can be cut and shaped without hurting the animal. On flat land, horse hooves wear down evenly, but on stony ground, hooves split and break, while on soft ground, hooves grow long and diseased. A horse receives regular attention from a "farrier," a person trained to look after hooves and fit protective metal shoes. The hoof consists of the outer "wall," the "sole," and wedge-shaped "frog."

Old horseshoe and nails just removed from horse's hoof by farrier

1 Remove old shoe
The horse stands patiently while the farrier carefully levers off the worn old shoe.

Indian shoes
Methods of shoeing horses have been the same worldwide for centuries. In this drawing, three workers are shoeing a horse during the time of the Mogul emperors in northern India, c. 1600 CE.

Girth's powerful muscles enable horse to do very heavy work

Feathering on foot

Shoeing a four-year-old Shire horse

Farrier's box of essential tools for shoeing horses

Good luck
A horseshoe is a lucky talisman. It is held with the open part at the top, so good luck does not drop out. Horseshoe pitching—a game of luck—is played in the US and Canada.

"Horn", or horseshoe-shaped excess hoof growth, removed by farrier

2 Hoof clean
The excess hoof is clipped and the hoof is filed and cleaned so it is ready for the new shoe.

3 At the forge
The farrier makes a new iron shoe at the forge. Using a heavy hammer, the farrier shapes the shoe on an anvil and adds holes for the nails.

4 Steaming
At the stables, the shoe is reheated, pressed onto the hoof to check the fit, and then allowed to cool down. The hoof gives off a smell of burning hair and much smoke, but this does not hurt the horse.

Height at withers 17.2 hh/ 70 in (178 cm)

Chestnut

6 Finished foot
The foot rim is filed before the farrier hammers it flat. Nails must be flush with the shoe, and the hoof and the outer shoe edge should match.

Filing hoof and nail ends flat

Balancing on one front foot

5 Nailing on the shoe
The farrier hammers special iron nails through predrilled holes in the shoe. Nail ends showing through the hoof are wrung off and turned back.

When "hippo" meant "horse"
Before iron horseshoes, the Romans tied a shoe of wicker or metal to the hoof with leather, called a "hipposandal" (hippo in Greek means "horse").

Hipposandal, French, 1st–3rd century CE

Bits and pieces

The earliest domestic horses and asses were ridden bareback and guided by a rope tied around the lower jaw. This is still the way to control donkeys in Turkey and Greece. The first bits, or bridles' mouthpieces with fastenings at each end to which reins are attached, were made of hide, bone, or wood. In about 1500 BCE, bronze and then iron replaced them. Until late Roman times, horsemen rode bareback. There were no saddles or stirrups (loops suspended from a saddle to support the rider's foot) in Europe until the 8th century CE. This didn't stop Eurasian or Native American horsemen from shooting arrows from a galloping horse. The most powerful ancient nomadic horsemen were the Scythians of Central Asia in the 4th century BCE.

Back view of woman riding sidesaddle

Jingle bells
Bells on the harness were a safety feature. If riders got lost, the chimes could be heard by rescuers.

Spurred on
Horses in 13th-century Europe had a hard time, for they were bridled with bits and goaded by armored knights wearing cruel spurs (U-shaped devices attached to the rider's boot heel).

Rowel spur (length 9 in/23 cm), made of iron and brass, western European, early 1500s

Rowel

Screw would have clamped stirrup to outside of shoe

Metal part of stirrup would have fit inside heel of shoe

Tiny rowel spur (length 1½ in/4 cm), made of iron and fitting directly onto shoe, European, late 1600s

Buckle for attaching stirrup to boot

Metal part of stirrup for "pricking" horse

Prick spur (total length 11 in/29 cm), made of iron, Moorish, early 1800s

Putting your foot in it
The Chinese probably invented metal foot stirrups in the 5th century CE. Stirrups spread westward to Europe. They influenced the battlefield, allowing horsemen to wield their weapons without falling off.

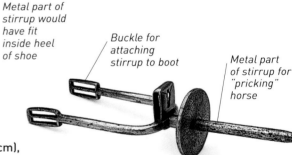

Brass fretwork

Dragon decoration

Box stirrup, made of painted wood and brass fretwork, French or Italian, late 1700s

Iron stirrup, Bulgar, 800–900 CE

Decorated boot stirrup, made of iron, Spanish, 1600s

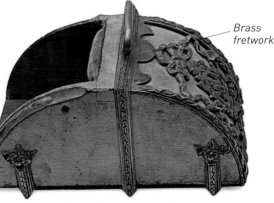

Brass stirrup, decorated with two dragons, Chinese, 1800s

Build a better bit
Three types of bit control domesticated horses. The first is the simple "snaffle" bit, developed into a jointed mouthpiece in Assyria, c. 900 BCE. A "curb" bit is unjointed with a chain under the horse's chin, which applies pressure with reins. A "pelham" bit combines two bits of a double bridle in one.

Joint

Rein ring

Jointed snaffle bit, Irish, 100 BCE–100 CE

Detail from the Bayeux tapestry from France, c. 1080

Defeat in battle
In the Battle of Hastings, 1066 CE, William the Conqueror's troops beat the English. One reason for victory was their use of stirrups, while the English dismounted to fight on foot.

Joint

Rein ring

Cheekpiece

Jointed snaffle bit with cheekpiece, Bulgar, 800–900 CE

Double rollers in horse's mouth

Curb chain

Brass boss

Rein ring

Curb bit made of steel and brass, European, 1500s

Brass boss

Curb chain

Rein ring

Mouthpiece

Curb bit made of steel and brass, Portuguese, 1800s

Brow band

Headpiece

Throatlatch

Height at withers 17 hh/ 68 in (173 cm)

Rein

Bit

Sidesaddle
This gray Lipizzaner gelding is being ridden sidesaddle. Women today usually only ride like this in the show ring or out hunting. In former times, from the early 1300s onward, the sidesaddle was the only way a female rider, wearing long, heavy skirts, could be mounted on a horse.

Girth

Safety stirrup

Rider on leather saddle made-to-measure in 1890

Woman, in Victorian dress, riding sidesaddle on a six-year-old Lipizzaner

Rein ring (terret), English, 1st century CE

Strap-union made of bronze (for joining straps together), English, 1st century CE

Decorated terret (a ring on saddle harness through which driving reins pass), found in Egypt, 1st century BCE

Exploring by horse

Without the horse, human history would have been very different. Civilizations would have evolved in their places of origin and people could not have explored and conquered. An invading force must have fast transportation and efficient movement of goods, weapons, and food, otherwise it is powerless against the defenses of settled communities. Although horseriding was the common form of transportation from 1000 BCE, it wasn't until the 11th century CE that horses were shod and saddles and stirrups used. From this time, the horse became important in war, sports, and travel.

Viking chessman
This 12th-century knight on horseback carving is one of the famous chessmen from Scotland's Isle of Lewis.

Genghis Khan
Genghis Khan (1162–1227 CE), the Mongolian conqueror, ruled an empire of nomadic horsemen that stretched across Asia into Europe

Statue of Charlemagne, the Holy Roman Emperor

Pair of bronze Etruscan riders, c. 500 BCE

Archers of the ancient world
These two Etruscan bronzes from Italy show how Scythian archers shot arrows from galloping horses. The archer shooting backward exemplifies the "Parthian shot," a technique used by nomadic horsemen on the steppes of central Asia.

Holy Roman Emperor
Charlemagne, or Charles the Great (742–814 CE), was the most famous ruler of the Middle Ages. In 796 CE, he led 15,000 horsemen against the Avars in Hungary, and later became Emperor of the Holy Roman Empire.

Fretwork

In the saddle
This 18th-century wooden saddle is probably similar to the one used by Genghis Khan 600 years before.

Tree

Cantle

Pommel

18th-century Tibetan saddle

Alexander the Great

Bucephalus, a black stallion born c. 331 BCE, is probably the most famous horse to have ever lived. He belonged to Alexander the Great (356–323 BCE), and together they conquered much of the known world—from Greece to Egypt and Afghanistan.

Stone frieze of Alexander the Great on his horse, Bucephalus (left), on a sarcophagus in Syria

Patron saint

St. George is England and Portugal's patron saint.

Archer showing "Parthian shot"

Tassel on bridle

Curb ring

Curb chain

Gold embroidery on felt, stitched onto leather backing

Golden wonder

This exquisite gold model of a four-horse chariot, c. 5th century BCE, is from the Achaemenid Empire of Persia (now Iran).

Part of treasure found near the Oxus River in central Asia

Reins

Early 19th-century North African bridle with curb bit

Fine hats
America's Sioux chieftains ride their most beautiful horses for ceremonial occasions.

To the Americas

Before 1492, when European settlers arrived in North and South America, the continents were inhabited by native people, who had arrived about 15,000 years earlier. European invaders had fast horses and mules, and they conquered the land. A few horses escaped to live and breed in the wild, and a century later, they had spread over the grasslands. Native Americans soon saw the value of the horse. They bartered with the Spanish for their own stock and learned to ride like the ancient horsemen.

The Black Hawk war
The Sauk Indians prized horses for war, hunting, and transportation. US officials made Keokuk (above, c. 1760–1848) Sauk chief and he signed treaties giving away Sauk land. Black Hawk, the Sauks' true leader defended the land, but was defeated. Millions of acres of Indian territory were ceded to the whites.

Beasts of burden
Before there were railroads across North America, teams of mules would haul heavy wagons along muddy roads that were impassable by other means of transportation.

Blaze

Central wooden shaft, or "tongue," to which harness is attached

Martingale

Stocking

Shod hoof gives better grip

Down Mexico way
In the early 1500s, Spanish conquistadors took horses to the New World, where they had been extinct for 10,000 years. Here Indians give Mexican conqueror Hernando Cortés (1485–1547) a necklace.

Westward, ho!

Trappers, traders, and missionaries were the first to reach the Pacific, but in 1843 a determined band of 1,000 settlers left Missouri on the 2,000-mile (3,300-km) trek westward along the Oregon Trail. Finally, after many grueling months, they reached their destination.

Canvas held up by iron hoop underneath

Waterproof heavy-duty canvas top

Brake lever

Axle supporting the weight of wagon and load

Iron rim over wooden wheel

Whippletree, attaching harness to wagon

Metal hub

Trace

Pair of Gelderlanders, 16.2 hh/66 in (168 cm)

Mobile home

Early European settlers traveled across North America in a covered wagon, or "prairie schooner." They had to be entirely self-sufficient, knowing how to shoe a horse, mend a wheel, and bake bread.

Front wheel, 4 ft (123 cm) across, is smaller for sharp turns

Cowboys

The horsemen, or gauchos, of the South American pampas work on huge ranches. They spend their lives in the saddle.

Running wild

There are no longer any truly wild horses, but all over the world there are many herds of horses and ponies described as "feral." These feral animals are descended from domesticated stock, but they live and breed in the wild. The last truly wild horses were the Przewalski's horses that survived in Mongolia until the 1960s. In North and South America, horses spread rapidly over the grasslands after the first Europeans brought horses and donkeys in the 15th century. Soon large herds of horses and donkeys were living wild all over the grassland and deserts.

Long ears

Well-proportioned head

Coat colors vary from bay, brown, and gray, but never piebald or skewbald

Strong legs support sturdy, well-built body

Well-formed feet with strong horn

Fell ponies
In Britain many breeds of pony live on the moors, like the Fell pony. Although Fell ponies are owned, they can live and breed with little human control.

German Dülmen
These rare ponies live semi-wild on the Duke of Croy's estate in Westphalia, Germany. They have been crossbred with British and Polish ponies, so are not purebred. The herd dates back to the 1300s.

The brumby of Australia
There have been feral horses in Australia for 150 years, since they were abandoned during the gold rush. Called brumbies, these horses reproduced in large numbers over vast areas. Since the 1960s, they have been hunted to such an extent that there are now very few of them.

Symbolic horses

A wild running horse has often been used as a symbol of freedom and elegance. It has advertised many things, from banks to sports cars—such as Mustang in the US, and Ferrari, the supreme speedster.

The mustangs of America

The feral horses, or mustangs, of the Nevada desert have hard lives traveling far and wide in search of grass and water.

Dawn in the Camargue

The beautiful white horses from the Camargue in the south of France have lived wild in the marshes of the Rhône delta for over 1,000 years. They have very wide hooves, adapted for life on wet grassland.

Star

Short stripe on face

Long, straight, full mane

Snip

Deep girth

Full forelock

New Forest ponies range from 12.2 to 14.2 hh/50–58 in (127–147 cm).

Blaze

The ponies of the New Forest

Herds of ponies have lived in the New Forest woodlands of Hampshire, England, since the 11th century. For 800 years, these ponies lived wild, but in the 19th century efforts were made to improve them by bringing in stallions of other breeds. They still run wild here, but are also reared on stud farms and used as riding ponies.

Horses of the world

Breeds of horse are often divided by breeders into three types. First are "hotbloods"—the Arab and Thoroughbred breeds. This name is a result of their descent from the Arab and Barb breeds of hot countries in North Africa and Arabia. Second are "coldbloods," which are the heavy draft horses of cold, northern climates. Third are "warmbloods," which are crosses between hotbloods and coldbloods. This group supplies most modern sports horses, except racehorses, which are Thoroughbreds. All Thoroughbreds can trace their ancestry to three stallions: Byerly Turk (c. 1689), Darley Arabian (c. 1702), and Godolphin Arabian (c. 1731).

Gray coat is black skin, with a mixture of white and black hairs, as in this Connemara pony from Ireland.

Dapple-gray occurs when dark gray hairs form rings on a gray coat, as in this Orlov Trotter from Russia.

Palomino (a color, not a breed) is a gold coat, as in this Haflinger pony from Austria.

Chestnut occurs in various shades of gold— from pale gold to a rich, red gold, as in this French Trotter from Normandy in France.

Bay is a reddish coat, with black mane, tail, and "points" (ears, legs, and muzzle), as in this Cleveland Bay from England.

Coronet is white hair just above the hoof.

Sock is the white hair reaching halfway up the cannon bone.

Stocking is the white hair reaching up to the knee, or hock.

Brown is mixed black and brown in coat, with brown mane, as in this Nonius from Hungary.

Decorated bridle

Height at withers 14.3 hh/59 in (150 cm)

Four-year-old, purebred Arab, mahogany bay in color

Moroccan horsemen ride at a festival

Barbs and Berbers
The Barb, second only to the Arab as the first horse breed, is the traditional mount of North African tribesmen, called Berbers.

Rearing up
Because horses are beautiful and can be easily trained, they are used in circus shows, where they can show unusual movements with their bodies.

Height at withers 14.1 hh/ 57 in (145 cm)

Coats of many colors
In this painting by Indian artists from the Mogul school (c. 1590), a crow addresses an assembly of animals in a Persian fable. The horses' coat colors are chestnut, light and dappled grays, bay, and skewbald.

15-year-old Arab, very light gray color with tiny dapples in coat

Horse fair
Horses have been sold at horse sales for centuries, as shown in this detail of a painting by English artist John Herring (1795–1865).

Aristocratic Arab
The Arab is the aristocrat of horses, with an elegant head, slender limbs, and fiery nature. Arabs have been carefully bred, and records kept of their pedigrees in both North Africa and Arabia.

Embroidered saddle-cloth

Other breeds and colors

Every country has its own breed of horse, adapted to life in its place of origin. Breeds are defined by their "conformation," or size and body shape, as well as color and any white markings on the face and legs. Horses come in different sizes—from the smallest horse, the Falabella, which measures 7.2 hh/30 in (76 cm) at the withers, to the largest breed, the Shire horse. A Shire stallion stands 16.2 hh/66 in (168 cm) and weighs about a ton. Many sayings link horse behavior to coat colors. There is an Arab saying that all horses but bays are unlucky, unless they have white markings, and another that a white horse is the most princely, but suffers in heat.

Height at withers 16.1 hh/65 in (165 cm)

Flat metal stirrup

Stars...
It is usual for horses to have white facial markings, such as a regular, or irregular, "star" shape high on the face. An example is this Danish Warmblood, a breed now regarded as Denmark's national horse.

... And stripes
A strip of white, extending from above the eyes to the nostrils, is called a "stripe," as on this Oldenburg, a breed established in Germany in the 1600s.

What the blazes!
A wide strip above the eyes and extending down the muzzle is a "blaze," as on this Gelderlander from the Netherlands. When white hair covers almost all the face, it is called a "white face."

Seven-year-old, dark gray, purebred Andalusian ridden by a woman in classical Spanish riding costume

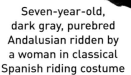

Classical equitation
The Spanish Riding School was founded in 1572 with Lipizzaner horses.

Horses in art

The beauty and strength of the horse has inspired sculptors and artists for thousands of years, such as this stylized work by German painter, Franz Marc (1880–1916).

The "Spanish Horse"

Known as the "Spanish Horse" for centuries, Andalusian horses were first bred by Carthusian monks at Spanish monasteries in the 1400s. Today's horses are bay or gray, but they were originally chestnut or black.

Numnah (sheepskin pad to protect horse's back)

Spanish-style saddle blanket

Exhibiting spectacular passage, a slow-tempo trot with exaggerated elevation of legs

Horses are called black when the coat, mane, tail, and legs are completely black, as in this Friesian from the Netherlands.

Roan color can be "strawberry" (where the coat color is chestnut with white hairs mixed), or "blue" (a black or brown coat with some white hair), as in this Italian Heavy Draft horse from Italy.

Dun color can be a blue, mouse, or light yellow coat (with black in the legs, mane, and tail), as in this Norwegian Fjord pony. The "dorsal eel stripe" seen on the mane and back is typical of this breed.

A spotted coat can have five varieties of pattern, usually dark spots on light hair, as seen here in this minute Falabella, first bred in Argentina.

Skewbald means white patches on another coat color. This Pinto pony has a chestnut coat with white patches ("Ovaro"), but a white coat with colored patches is called "Tobiano."

Piebald means large, irregular patches of white and black hairs in the coat, as in this Shetland pony.

War horses

The horse and the ass have been used by people to assist in wars for 5,000 years. By riding in chariots harnessed to a pair of horses, men could travel fast and cause damage to the enemy. Minor squabbles between individuals became battles as families expanded and villages were settled. When armed horseriders (cavalry) arrived at the time of Alexander the Great, the horse played a big role in all wars until after World War I, when mechanized vehicles took over. As higher, steady saddles were introduced, longer weapons could easily be used on the battlefield.

Napoleon's favorite
Marengo was the white Arab pony ridden by French leader, Napoleon Bonaparte (1769–1821) at the Battle of Waterloo in Belgium in 1815, when he was defeated by the British.

Rider's uniform embroidered with real gold thread

Made of pure silver, these drums weigh 150 lb (68 kg)

Royal coat of arms (featuring a lion and a unicorn) embroidered with gold and silver threads on damask silk of drum banner

Bridle's beard, or tussle, made of natural horse hair—black hair surrounding dyed red hair

Double reins covered with real gold thread— boot reins connected to rider's stirrups, second set to rider's waist

Drum horse
Today the drum horse is used during processions, but in the past, the beating of drums and the blowing of trumpets gave men courage as they went into battle. These drums were given by King William IV of England to the Life Guards regiment of his Household Cavalry in 1830.

Tilting at windmills
In 1605, Spanish poet Miguel de Cervantes (1547–1616) created his memorable character, Don Quixote, and his mare, Rocinante. He and his donkey-riding friend used lances to attack "giants," which were really windmills.

15-year-old, blue roan Clydesdale carrying drums and rider, from the Household Cavalry of Queen Elizabeth II of Great Britain and the Commonwealth

Red Cross flag on World War I ambulance

Whippletree to which horse's harness was hitched to vehicle

The first ambulances were harnessed to a pair of horses or mules.

Brake

Small front wheel to allow sharp turning

Large rear wheel to carry heavy loads

Into battle

The Charge of the Light Brigade was the most disastrous battle of the Crimean War (1853–1856), with huge casualties of horses and men.

Tibetan warrior

For centuries, the Tibetan cavalry used armor made of small metal plates (lamellae) laced with leather thongs. This armor, for horse and rider, was used by the nomadic warriors of central Asia. The Tibetans have preserved this armor.

Metal shaffron to protect head

Crinet to protect neck

Peytral to protect breast

Leather lace

Small metal plate

Protective crupper

Tibetan cavalry armor, used from the 17th to 19th centuries

Australian artillery

The Waler (named after New South Wales in Australia where horses were first imported 200 years ago) was the finest cavalry horse during World War I. These horses were strong and hardy, able to carry heavy loads, and had good stamina.

19th-century British cavalry spur, made of nickel silver

Sturdy stirrups

The stirrup was the most important innovation in the history of the horse in war because it enabled a heavily armed rider to stay on his horse.

Ghanaian warrior

This brass model of a warrior on horseback was cast in Ghana in West Africa during the 18th century.

War necessities

Pack horses and mules hauled essential supplies of food, water, and arms to the Front Line.

Whippletree

Tongue

Metal barrel containing water for troops or animals

World War I water wagon, made in England, used in France, hauled by two horses

The age of chivalry

From the 11th century European politics was dominated by the feudal system. Knights were feudal lords who owned land and controlled serfs. These knights were Christians, bound by the religious and moral code of chivalry. The ideal knight was brave and courteous, and dedicated to war against non-Christians. By 1200, much of Europe was settled under feudalism and knights began the conquest of new lands. The Crusades were fought over territory, and the code of chivalry meant that leaders could depend on knights to die for the cause of winning Jerusalem from the Muslims.

Samurai warrior
This painting depicts a 12th-century Japanese samurai warrior in battle. The honorable samurai was totally loyal to his feudal lord.

European, late-19th-century brass copy of 15th-century medieval spur with rowel, which was long to reach under the horse's armor

Lambrequin, or mantling

Leather gauntlet, or glove

Blunted wooden lance

Cloth surcoat

Caparison, or decorated horse covering

Mail armor

The romance of the joust
The armed knights learned how to fight on horseback in competitive tournaments. This sport, known as "jousting" (from the Latin *juxtare*, meaning to meet together), was part of the code of chivalry. Knights tried to win points by either unhorsing their opponents or breaking their lances against the others' shields. From the dangerous hand-to-hand fighting, or mêlées, of the 12th century to the colorful pageantry of the 15th and 16th centuries, these tournaments were popular spectator sports.

Reconstruction of a pair of sporting jousters from the early 14th century

Armor fit for a king

Henry VIII of England passed laws to increase horse size by preventing breeding by small stock. As the cannon became the new weapon of choice, armor was no defense, but it was still used in royal parades.

Bronze eye-guard for protecting a horse's face, English, 1st century CE

This full horse armor (or bard), known as the "Burgundian Bard," was given by Emperor Maximilian I of Germany to Henry VIII c. 1515.

Full metal shaffron

This 16th-century Turkish shaffron (head defense for a horse) was made of gilt-copper, or "tombak." It was part of a monument to the Ottoman Empire (1200s to 1900s).

Metal helm

Wooden, or leather, crest in the form of a bird or animal was sometimes worn here

Vamplate, or metal disk, for protecting hand

Leg guard

This wooden German jousting saddle (c. 1500) was used in a "joust of peace" with blunted lances. Two bows curved round the knight's thighs to protect his limbs.

Pelham bit

Shield painted in heraldic colors, repeated on horse's caparison

Coeur de Lion

Richard the Lionheart (1157–1199) became king of England in 1189. He found fame by bravely leading the Third Crusade to Palestine.

Painful stop

Four-spiked iron caltrops were put in the ground to lame the enemy's horses as they stepped on them.

Traveling by horse

Horses, asses, and mules have transported people and goods for more than 4,000 years. The first harness and carts were made of wood, bone, and leather, until 3,500 years ago when copper and bronze were used on chariots, followed by iron 1,000 years later. Metal additions to harnesses speeded up travel times in southern Europe and Asia. But in rainy northern Europe, the pack horse remained the best mode of travel until roads were built by the Romans and built again in the Middle Ages (1100–1500 CE).

Fit for a queen
This is a replica of Queen Elizabeth I's carriage—the first carriage to be built for the British monarchy. Until then, royalty rode in carts. With steps folded up the side, the carriage's padded roof protected against rain.

Highwayman and horse
Dick Turpin (1705–1739) was a legendary English highwayman who, it has been recorded, rode to the city of York in record time on his mount Black Bess.

Horse feathers
The horses of Native Americans had endurance and stamina for war and hunts. Decoration was part of Native American culture. Chiefs wore bright colorful feathered headdresses and adorned their horses, too.

Bareback rider!
In 11th-century legend, Lady Godiva rode naked through Coventry, UK

Blinker

Blaze

Bit with a straight bar

Collar

Metal hame with twist at top as traditional Romany decoration

Breeching strap

Beast of burden
This stone frieze shows that the ancient Assyrians bred powerful mules to carry hunting gear.

The travelers
For many centuries, Romany gypsies have traveled around Europe in their caravans. No one knows where they came from, but they may be of Hindu origin.

Patron saint
St. Christopher (3rd century CE) was patron saint of travelers—his feast day is July 25.

18th-century bronze horse and rider from Nigeria in West Africa

Pilgrims' progress
Pilgrim riders featured in the *Canterbury Tales* by poet Geoffrey Chaucer.

Canvas-covered barrel top

Shaft

Sock

Nine-year-old Irish Draft horse (wearing traditional Romany harness) pulling a gypsy caravan, built in Ireland, c. 1850

Horse-drawn vehicles

Snow sled with fur-lined seats, built in the Netherlands, c. 1880

Elegant and expensive carriage harnessed to a pair of beautiful horses

Early chariots in the ancient world had solid wooden wheels and a fixed axle that did not pivot. The invention of light, spoked wheels allowed chariots to travel faster. The four-wheeled carriage, with a swiveling axle that could turn independently, was a feature by the early Middle Ages. The poor traveled in carts and on horse buses, while the rich traveled in grand carriages harnessed to majestic horses. Care went into maintaining horses, harness, and carriages. Horses were fed and fitted with shoes, wheels were greased and repaired, and carriages were kept clean and dry.

Bronze model of horse and carriage, Easte Han Dynasty, China, second century CE

American ambush

Early European immigrants who traveled across North America by stagecoach were often attacked by mounted Native Americans, armed with stolen guns.

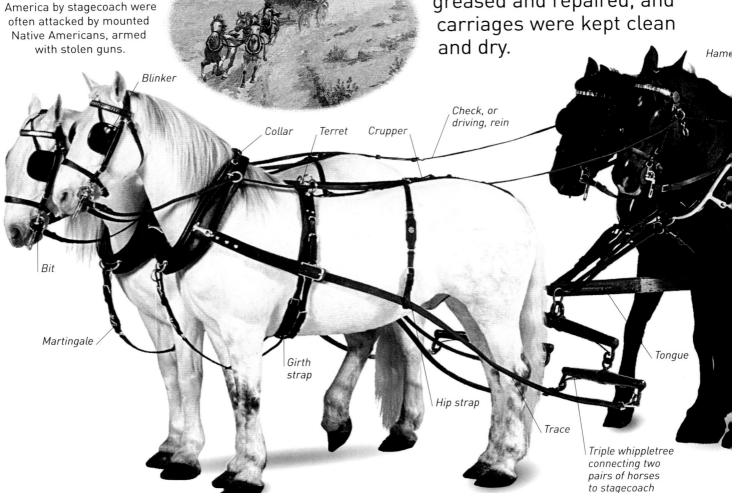

Blinker

Collar

Terret

Crupper

Check, or driving, rein

Ham

Bit

Martingale

Girth strap

Hip strap

Tongue

Trace

Triple whippletree connecting two pairs of horses to stagecoach

Only one seat left on this overcrowded horse bus—two people will be disappointed

Driver's seat

Seating for two passengers

A type of Victorian carriage called a barouche, made in England from a French design, c. 1880

Way out West

Two Americans—Henry Wells (1805–1878) and William Fargo (1818–1881)—opened banking and shipping services in San Francisco in 1852, linking the far West with the rest of the nation. The Wells Fargo stagecoaches carried passengers, money, and valuables.

Two sets of reins connecting the two pairs to driver

"Jehu," or driver

Guard-messenger riding shotgun

Brake lever controlled by driver's foot

Extra luggage stowed on top

Roll-up leather curtains to let in cool air, or to keep out snow and rain

Seating inside for nine passengers

Passengers' luggage stowed in rear trunk

WELLS FARGO & CO. OVERLAND STAGE

U.S. MAIL

Step for passengers getting into stagecoach

Box under driver's seat containing tools, water bucket, mail pouches, and strongboxes full of valuables

Two pairs of Welsh Cobs hauling Wells Fargo stagecoach, made in the US, late 1800s

Standing room for 12 passengers

Driver's seat

Hunting brake, with driver's seat and space for standing room only, made in England, c. 1880

Heavy horses

In Europe and Asia, "the age of the horse" lasted from the classical times of Greece and Rome until the start of the 19th century when they were overtaken by the steam engine. Until then, the horse, mule, and donkey were the main means of transportation and essential to agricultural work. They were used in forestry, harvesting, threshing on the land, and drawing water from wells. In the damp soil of northern Europe, powerful heavy horses were needed to plow and haul. Today Europe's heavy horses are exported worldwide.

Haymaking in Ireland
The horse and the donkey are still used on small farms in Ireland. Here a wagon is being loaded with hay, which is winter food for the farm animals.

Long, arched neck with thick mane

Fine head with straight profile

Belgian compact
Also called Brabant, this ancient breed of heavy draft horses from Belgium is pure-bred. They are still used on farms in the US.

Decorated mane

Horse brass

Hame, on heavy collar

Broad, deep-chested body

Chestnut-colored Belgian Draft horse

Before the tractor
The invention of the rigid, padded horse collar by the Chinese, c. 500 CE, spread across Asia to Europe. This impacted on agriculture, as horse-drawn plows became the tractors of their day. Today plowing with horses is slower than using a tractor, but it is better for the land. Plowing competitions take place at agricultural shows in Britain and Europe.

Strong, muscular leg

No feathering on heel of foot

Dapple-gray Percheron

Bridle   Collar

Saddle

Hip strap

Breech band

Loin strap   Chain trace

Mountain climber

The Avelignese is raised in in the mountains of Italy. Used as both a draft horse and a pack horse, it measures up to 14.3 hh/59 in (150 cm).

Chestnut-colored Avelignese

Gray-colored Boulonnais

A better brew

n about 1800, the horse became mportant in the brewing industry. rewers had horses, drays, and arts, as well as a blacksmith nd wheelwright. Horses were lso used for grinding the malt nd for driving water pumps.

Chestnut-colored Suffolk Punch

French pride

The head of the Boulonnais—a native of northwest France, like the Percheron— shows the influence of its Arab ancestry. This silky-coated ancient breed stands over 16 hh/64 in (163 cm).

A powerful punch

The Suffolk Punch was developed as a farm horse in Suffolk, England, in the late 1700s. Not only does it have fantastic stamina and power, but it also needs less food than other heavy breeds. The Suffolk's coat coloring is always chestnut.

Long, powerful indquarters

est of France

he Percheron from orthern France the best known reed of heavy horse. s elegance, from rossbreeding with rab stallions, has ade it a popular reed in the US nd Canada.

After the harvest is done

Every fall horses help ready the ground for new crops after the harvest. Horses are plowing and harrowing in this 16th-century Flemish scene.

Deep in the forest

Heavy horses have traditionally been used to haul heavy logs from forests.

Horse-drawn rake for gathering cut hay into long, smooth rows

Horse power

Without the horse, the Industrial Revolution could never have happened. Horse transportation enabled manufactured goods to be carried to ships for export abroad and enabled people to flock to cities for industrial work. Factory horses provided power to engines and machines for grinding malt and wheat, spinning cotton, or furnace blowing. Ponies were sent down into mines to haul loads of coal and also towed coal-filled barges along canals. Machinery has now replaced horses, but the term used to measure an engine's pulling power is still "horsepower."

Cog

Horse buses
The first public horse carriages in Britain started in 1564, but roads were so bad that people could not go far.

Weighing scales

COAL MERCHANT
THOMAS JEWELL

Heavily laden coal wagon, made in England, 1920

Shaft attached to grinding stones

Snowshoes
In heavy snow, sure-footed horses are needed to haul logs out of forests, or sleds full of goods, like these Haflinger ponies in Bavaria in southern Germany.

Brake

Sack of coal

Lamp

Horn

Exploring the interior
Horses hauled wooden wagons loaded with supplies to Australia's interior. Wagon safety depended upon the correct wheels.

Water hose

LONDON

Water bucket

Victorian fire engine, English, 1890—wide wheels let horses turn corners without any spills

Giant iron fly-wheel attached to an iron rod, or shaft

Around in circles
The tediousness of this circular work is all the more apparent when viewed from above.

Heavy collar

Whippletree attached to iron bar, in turn linked to shaft

Metal linked-chain trace

Long, muscled leg helping horse pull heavy load

Huge, flat grinding stones hidden underground

Shire horse pulling heavy horse gin, or horsewheel, inside a circular building called a roundhouse

Towing a barge
Horses and mules were often used to pull barges heavily laden with coal or farm produce along rivers and canals in Britain and Europe, right up until the 20th century.

A hard grind
This horse is being used to turn a mill wheel to grind corn into flour—just as horses, mules, and donkeys have done across Europe since Roman times. Animals were forced to walk around in a small circle for hours, pulling the rope or chain that turned the heavy grinding stone. Sometimes, a pair of horses would carry out this operation.

Light draft work

The common light draft horse was the mainstay of global transportation until the steam engine was invented in the 1820s. Light draft horses were powerful and fast, pulling wagons, carriages, and carts. They did not belong to a particular breed, but some, like the Cleveland Bay of Yorkshire, had been preserved as purebreeds since ancient times. Cleveland Bays were called "Chapman horses" because they carried the loads of traveling salesmen ("chapmen") around the countryside.

Hansom cab (c. 1850), driven by single driver and horse

Feathered plume

Crowd control
The specially trained horses of mounted police still perform an important function in moving fast through crowds. They give their riders mobility and a good view of events.

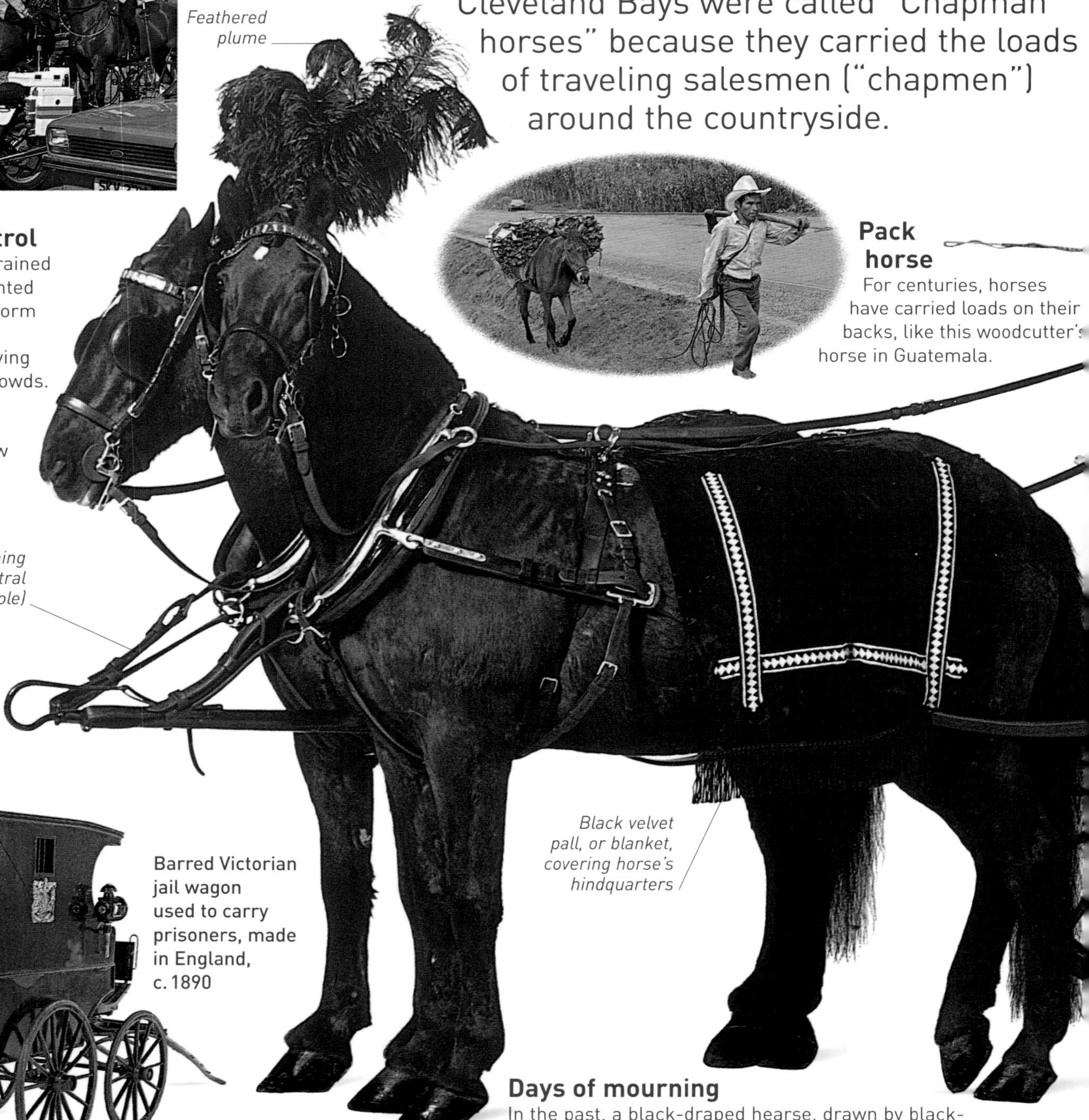

Pack horse
For centuries, horses have carried loads on their backs, like this woodcutter's horse in Guatemala.

Pole strap attaching collar to central shaft (pole)

Royal coat of arms

Barred Victorian jail wagon used to carry prisoners, made in England, c. 1890

Black velvet pall, or blanket, covering horse's hindquarters

Days of mourning
In the past, a black-draped hearse, drawn by black-plumed horses, slowly carried a coffin to a funeral.

Sunday morning drive

This 19th-century print of a family outing in a horse-drawn carriage is by American lithographers Nathaniel Currier and James Ives.

Harness attached to center pole

Pair of grays and phaeton, English, c. 1840

Man about town

In English spa towns in the early 19th century, young gentlemen dashed around town in elegant sporting phaetons, driven with the top up or down.

Driver dressed in dark mourning suit

Plumes made of ostrich feathers

Coffin

Engraved glass sides

Splinter bar to which traces are attached

Pair of black Welsh Cobs, in black and silver harness, pulling funeral hearse, made in England, c. 1850

R. JORDAN & SONS

THE PADDOCK

Rubber-wheeled dairy wagon, made in England, c. 1950

North American equids

Indigenous wild horses of North America became extinct 10,000 years ago. Domestic horses arrived with Christopher Columbus in 1492. Since then horses have symbolized freedom and enterprise in North America, and increased horse numbers matched that of humans. Horses have been steady companions, pulling heavy loads in desert heat, down dark mines, and along muddy roads. The horse gave Native Americans their fastest transportation.

Buffalo Bill
In 1882 rider Buffalo Bill Cody (1846–1917) held the first professional rodeo show at a Fourth of July festivities in Nebraska.

Travel today
The Amish settled in Pennsylvania in the 1700s, developing the Conestoga (a heavier version of the covered wagon) to explore the West. Their simple lifestyle sees them still using horses for work and travel.

A musical ride
The Royal Canadian Mounted Police are famous for the pageantry—red tunics and black horses—of their musical ride.

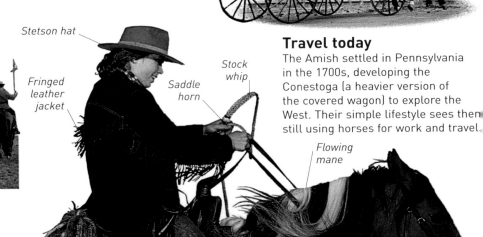

Stetson hat

Fringed leather jacket

Stock whip

Saddle horn

Flowing mane

Western curb bit

Leather chaps, or pants

Leather stirrups

Legendary ladies
Calamity Jane, Annie Oakley, Belle Starr... the list of female legends of the Old West is long, when cowgirls shot guns and rode horses. Outlaws, like Frank and Jesse James and Billy the Kid, were chased by lawmen like Wyatt Earp. They all rode horses.

The Appaloosa, with its distinctive spotted coat, was a favorite mount of Native Americans

Cowgirl in typical Western clothes riding a skewbald Cob

Stampede!

Every July at the Calgary Stampede in Canada, the contests of skill and speed at this rodeo include the dramatic chuck (food) wagon races. Two pairs of horses, a cook-driver, and four outriders race to be first across the finish line.

Hollywood heroes

"There isn't a bronc that can't be rode; there isn't a cowboy that can't be thrown." The bucking horse at the rodeo symbolizes man's need to subjugate the wild and free. Wild horse races feature at the rodeo, with unbroken horses ridden to show off the cowboys' courage. Movie cowboys and their horses, such as the Lone Ranger and Silver, helped to recreate the legend of the Old West.

Buffalo hunt

American artist George Catlin painted the Native Americans' horses hunting buffalo, which all but disappeared after being overhunted by European immigrants.

Paul Revere's ride

Famous for his night ride from Boston on April 18, 1775, to warn the colonists of Massachusetts that British troops were coming, Paul Revere (1735–1818) and his horse are American icons.

Army roughriders

Ordinary cavalrymen (an army's mounted forces) spent hours in the saddle, so strong horses were essential. American artist Frederic Remington painted the US Cavalry in hot pursuit.

Lasso for roping cattle

Stetson

Saddle horn

Silver and tooled leather gunbelt

Western curb bit

Leather chaps

Leather stirrups

Cowboy on Palomino (part Thoroughbred, part Arab)

Sporting horses

"They rapidly flew over the plain, swiftly... whilst their manes were tossed about by the breath of the wind." This description of a chariot race comes from Homer's *Iliad* (8th century BCE). Four-horse chariot races were part of the early Olympic Games, while centuries later, the Romans raced horses in special arenas. In the 11th century, the first flat racing began in England, before riding schools teaching classical equitation started in Europe. In 1750, the first Jockey Club was founded in England. Today, competitive sports with horses are as popular as ever.

Every year in Siena, Italy, horses and riders race around the main square in the exciting *Palio*

Circus horse by French painter Georges Seurat (1859–1891)

Pommel

Cantle

Metal stirrup

A smooth leather English saddle has a very low cantle and pommel.

Legend goes that Pelops drove a four-horse chariot to found the Olympic Games in 1222 BCE.

Hard hat

Format riding jacket

Throatlash

Running martingale

Browband

Cheekpiece

Noseband

Seven-year-old dapple-gray jumper—a mix of Irish Draft and Irish Thoroughbred

Numnah

Painted wooden barrier at least 4½ ft (1.4 m) high

Point to point
Steeplechasing began in 1752 as a cross-country race. A church steeple was the goal, and all the hedges or gates had to be jumped to reach it.

Over they go
To jump over obstacles in their path is part of the natural behavior of wild horses that are galloping away from a predator. But domesticated horses will onl[y] jump when directed to do so by their riders. To train a horse to be a show jumper is a long and complicated process.

In cold water

Three-day eventing tests the endurance, speed, and obedience of a horse, as well as its rider's ability. The event is broken down into dressage on the first day, followed by a cross-country/steeplechase course with a water hazard, and show jumping on the third and final day.

Saddle horn

High cantle

Lariat

Leather stirrup

Western leather saddles had pommels (saddle horns) used by cowboys to lasso cattle.

Fun for everyone

Mounted games, or gymkhanas, offer young riders a chance to see what they and their ponies can do at this junior level of equestrian, or horseriding, competition.

Riding sidesaddle began with European royalty about 600 years ago.

Rein

Classic jodhpurs, or riding pants

English jumping saddle

Bridoon

Tendon boots to protect from overreach of hind feet

Girth

Metal stirrup

Anyone for polo?

Polo was invented by the Chinese about 2,500 years ago. Today it is popular in Argentina, the US, Australia, and Britain. Two teams of four players each hit the ball with long-handled mallets and try to score as many goals as possible. The team with the most goals wins.

They're off!

Modern flat racing—racing on a track with no obstacles—owes its existence to the Thoroughbred, first developed in Britain in the 17th and 18th centuries.

Horseplay

The close bond that has been forged over thousands of years between humans and horses cannot be broken by the rise of the car. The horse is popular in competitive sports, and those who cannot take part in show jumping or racing can watch it on television. Most highly bred horses must be carefully trained to maintain their fitness and optimize their chance of winning. Racehorses use their natural instincts to follow the leading horses, helped by the sting of a whip. Show jumpers and dressage horses mix training with obedience. Horses provide sport and recreation, from pony-trekking and endurance racing to international driving and classical equitation.

Away at the races
Flat racing—the "Sport of Kings"—is popular around the world, with classic races like England's Derby, America's Belmont Stakes, and Australia's Melbourne Cup.

Height at withers 15 hh /60 in (152 cm)

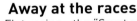

Creek crossing
Pony-trekking is a popular recreation for both adults and children. Here children are riding ponies in single file across a shallow stream in the Victorian Alps in southeastern Australia.

Pacers and trotters
In North America, France, Russia, and Australia, the trotting, or harness, race is as popular as flat racing. The modern trotting race is similar to ancient chariot races, except that it is a single trotting horse. In pacing, legs move in lateral (same side) pairs.

Horse race
For centuries, riders raced long-distance to break the latest time and distance records, as shown in this 18th-century Japanese print.

Three-year-old bay American Standardbred driven by owner in his racing colors

Elegant dressage
Classical riding, or dressage, shows the horse at the peak of its fitness and its obedience to its rider. It peaked in popularity during the 18th century. In modern advanced dressage competitions, marks out of 10 are given for excellence.

For centuries, horse's tail hair has been used to string musical instrument bows.

Hunters return
Hunting on horseback has been popular since the Assyrians, c. 2500 BCE, when prey was lions or wild oxen. Later, in Europe, as in this 16th-century Flemish calendar, the quarry was the stag, bear, or hare. By the 17th century, the English developed foxhunting, helped by trained scent hounds.

Driving test
At horse shows, driving events are popular. In 1970, the first international horse-driving trials took place. These trials had presentation and dressage on the first day, followed by a marathon of 17 miles (27 km), and then obstacle driving on the third day.

Driving whip

Jockey cap

Shirt showing owner's racing colors

Sulky, or cart

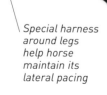

Special harness around legs help horse maintain its lateral pacing

Horse walk
The horse has four gaits—walk, trot, canter, and gallop. Walk has four beats—left hind, left fore, right hind, and right fore legs. Trot has two beats—left hind and right fore together, right hind and left fore together. Canter has three beats—left hind, left fore, and right hind together, and finally right fore leg. Gallop has four beats, the same as the walk, before all feet come off the ground.

Useful ponies

Children who learn to ride and look after a pony develop an understanding of the rich relationships that can exist between humans and animals. In the past, the native ponies of northern Europe were used as pack animals and for farmwork, and then, when a docile pony was too old to work, it was given to a child for riding lessons. At that time almost everyone could handle a horse. Today fewer people learn to ride and even fewer have a pony, but for those who do, it is a very rewarding experience.

Through all kinds of weather
Pony Express riders braved bad weather, tough terrain, and attacks by Native Americans to carry the post 2,000 miles (3,300 km) across the US in the 1860s.

Small but mighty
Shetland ponies were bred as farm animals and, despite their size, they can draw heavy carts.

Pair of black Shetland ponies hitched to a cart loaded with hay and a bag of feed

Straw for bedding

Riding for the disabled
Disabled people who want to ride should have the chance to do so. This rider directs her pony with her feet, by reins attached to the stirrups.

How to look after your pony

To be responsible for a pony is hard work, as the animal's welfare is dependent on its owner. The pony must have pasture, fresh water, shelter, exercise, and companionship. It must be groomed and inspected for parasites.

Nourishing mix of barley, oats, corn, pony nuts, Spanish beans, and molasses

Sugar beet (must be soaked for 12 or 24 hours before feeding)

A blue-glazed toy showing a boy and his pony, found in Egypt, dating to c. 200 CE

Rolled barley

Various types of rug or sheet are needed
to keep the horse warm in winter, or
protect it from flies in hot weather.

Dressage
whip

Lunge
whip

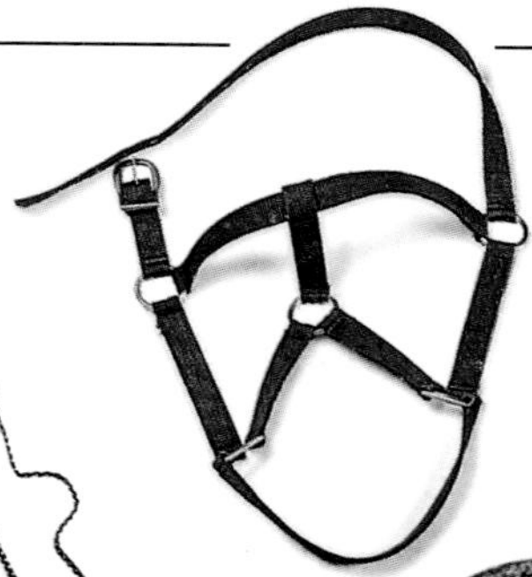

Headcollar
for training
horse to be
on the lead

Around and around
Every fairground has a merry-go-round,
or carousel, on which children can safely
ride a brightly painted mechanical horse.

Hoof pick

Molting
brush

Hoof oil

Curry comb
or removing
ried mud

Soft body brush

Metal comb used
when braiding

Hay for
eating

Miner's
lamp

Pit ponies
lind ponies were often taken to work down
coal mines because they did not need to
ee their way along the tunnels. It was wet,
old, and dark, with miners and ponies
ving underground for months on end.

A young boy and his blue roan
Shetland pony ready for working
underground in a coal mine

Three-tined fork for
mucking out stables

Did you know?

AMAZING FACTS

The head of this herd of horses is probably a mare

A horse drinks 6½ gallons (25 liters) of water a day—about 13 times more than a person.

Within an hour of being born, a foal can stand and walk. A child takes about a year to master the same skills. This ability is essential for the foal to move on with the herd.

A herd of horses is usually led by a mare (a female horse). She decides when the herd should move on to look for fresh grazing. She uses behavior like the bite threat to keep the herd in order.

The "horsepower" is an internationally recognized unit of the pulling power of an engine. Scientists define it as the power that is required to lift a weight of 165 lb (75 kg) over a distance of 39 in (1 m) in 1 second. A real horse is 10 to 13 times as strong as this.

People argued for years about whether a horse takes all four feet off the ground when it gallops. In 1872 photographer Eadweard Muybridge set up a line of 24 cameras and photographed a horse galloping past. The pictures proved a horse has all four feet off the ground.

A donkey carrying a load of straw

"Doing the donkey work" means doing hard, boring work. The expression comes from the fact that donkeys were bred for their stamina and endurance to carry heavy loads.

A mother horse and her foal

Horses have powerful lungs and strong hearts to help them run fast. A Thoroughbred's heart can weigh 11 lb (5 kg), which is 16 times heavier than an adult person's heart.

The Shire Horse is the largest breed of horse, but the biggest horse ever was a Percheron called Dr. Le Gear. He measured 21 hands (84 in/213 cm) high.

A 20-year-old horse shows its teeth

The expression "straight from the horse's mouth" means to hear something directly from the best source. It comes from the best way to discover the age of a horse, which is to examine its teeth. As a horse ages, its incisor teeth wear down and protrude much more.

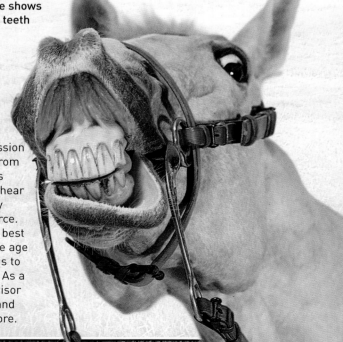
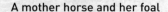

QUESTIONS AND ANSWERS

Q Why do newborn foals look so gangly?

A When a foal is born, its legs are already 90 percent of their adult length, whereas the rest of its body has to grow a lot. This makes it look gangly. Foals often bend their front legs to reach down to eat grass.

Q Why are horses' eyes positioned on the sides of their heads?

A This eye position gives the horse good all-around vision, which is vital for spotting potential dangers.

Q Why do horses often roll on the ground?

A Rolling helps a horse to scratch places it can't otherwise reach and to shed loose hairs from its coat. Each horse leaves its individual scent on the rolling patch. These scents mix together to produce a unique "herd smell" that helps the herd to bond.

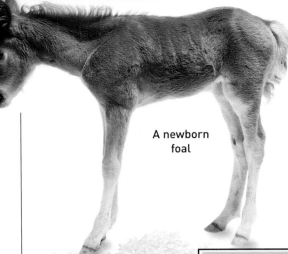

A newborn foal

Q How fast can a horse run?

A The maximum recorded speed for a galloping horse is 43 mph (69 kph). This puts the horse among the 10 fastest mammals in the world, but way behind the fastest animal, the cheetah, which tops 65 mph (105 kph).

A horse rolling

Q Why do horses run away?

A Horses facing danger have two options—fight or flight. They nearly always run away. One horse is always on guard. If it senses danger, it alerts the others and the herd all run off.

Q When was horse racing first invented?

A The first records of a ridden race come from the ancient Greek Olympic Games in 624 BCE. It took place over about 1,313 yd (1,200 m).

Q Why do horses come in so many different shapes and sizes?

A People have created different types of horse by selective breeding. This means limiting breeding to selected animals, by crossbreeding between horse types or inbreeding within a family. This can produce a specific skill, such as strength or speed. Distinctive breeds have emerged over time.

Q How did the Przewalski's horse get its unusual name?

A The Przewalski's horse is named after the man who discovered it—Nikolay Przhevalsky. This 19th-century Russian explorer traveled around eastern central Asia. His wildlife discoveries included the wild camel and wild horse, which he found in western Mongolia in the 1870s.

Record Breakers

HIGHEST JUMP
The world record for the highest horse jump is 8 ft 1.25 in (2.47 m) by Captain Alberto Larraguibel Morales riding Huaso.

SPEED RECORD
The fastest winner of the Epsom Derby was a horse named Workforce, who completed the 1.5-mile (2.4-km) course in just 2 minutes 31.33 seconds in 2010.

BIGGEST BREED
The largest breed of horse is the Shire Horse, which stands 16.2–17.2 hands (65–69 in/165–175 cm) high.

SMALLEST BREED
The smallest breed of horse is the Falabella, which is just 7.5 hands (30 in/76 cm) high.

Shire Horse

Falabella

Identifying breeds

There are about 160 different breeds and types of horse around the world. Many were developed for specific purposes.

PONIES

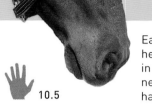

Each horse's height is given in hands, next to the hand symbol.

10.5

AMERICAN SHETLAND
This pony, from the Shetland Islands, was taken to the US in 1885.

10–12

CASPIAN
The Caspian is the most ancient horse breed, and an ancestor of the Arab horse.

13–14.2

CONNEMARA
Fast, courageous, and good at jumping, this Irish pony is ideal for competitions.

UP TO 13.3

HAFLINGER
The Austrian Haflinger pony is always chestnut or palomino in color with a distinctive flaxen mane and tail.

13–14

FJORD PONY
This Norwegian pony is used for riding, carrying loads, and pulling plows. Its mane is usually cut short.

UNDER 12

WELSH MOUNTAIN PONY
Thanks to its origins in the Welsh mountains, this hardy pony is able to survive on minimal rations.

RIDING HORSES

14.2–15.2

APPALOOSA
This horse has a distinctive spotted coat. It is descended from horses brought to the Americas by the Spanish conquistadors.

14.2–15

ARAB
The Arab is the purest breed of horse. It comes from the Arabian peninsula, where it was in existence as early as 2500 BCE.

14.2–15

BARB
This breed comes from Morocco, where it was the mount of the Berber horsemen. It is normally gray or black in color.

14.3–16

QUARTER HORSE
This was the first American breed of horse. It was used for farmwork and herding cattle and made a perfect cowboy's horse.

15.3–16

SELLE FRANÇAIS
This horse's name means "French saddle horse." It was bred for riding, and today is used for show jumping and racing.

16–16.2

THOROUGHBRED
This is the fastest and most valuable of all the breeds of horse. The Thoroughbred is used primarily for racing.

DRIVING HORSES

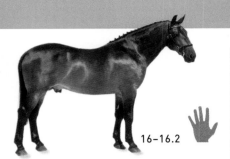

CLEVELAND BAY
Bred in the northeast of England, the Cleveland Bay was used to carry heavy men out hunting and to pull carriages.

16–16.2

15 AND OVER

FRIESIAN
This horse from the Netherlands was often used to pull funeral carriages because of its black color.

15.2–16.2

GELDERLANDER
Bred specifically to pull carriages, this Netherlands horse is often used in carriage-driving competitions.

15–15.3

HACKNEY
The British Hackney has a high-stepping gait. It was bred to pull carriages, especially the famous Hackney Cab.

15.1–16.2

LIPIZZANER
The white Lipizzaner horse is used at the Spanish Riding School in Vienna, where it excels at displays of dressage.

15.2

STANDARDBRED
This American horse is the world's best breed for harness racing. It can cover 1 mile (1.6 km) in under two minutes.

DRAFT HORSES

15–16

ARDENNAIS
Originating from the Ardennes region of France and Belgium, this is the oldest of the European heavy breeds.

16.2–17

BELGIAN DRAFT
This horse was originally bred for farmwork. It has relatively short legs, but great strength.

16.2

CLYDESDALE
The Clydesdale originates from Scotland. It was used for pulling heavy loads in cities, particularly brewers' drays.

16.2–17.2

SHIRE HORSE
The Shire Horse, from the middle shires of England, is the largest breed of horse. It was used on farms to pull plows, and in cities to pull brewers' drays.

16.2–17.2

PERCHERON
The French Percheron has been used for pulling coaches, farmwork, and riding.

Find out more

If you would like to get more involved in the world of horses, there are lots of ways to do it. You could visit a horse show or a county or state show where many breeds of horse are often on display. Why not try riding lessons? Once you have mastered the basics, you can go trekking in the countryside, or even enter a local competition.

Rosettes
Rosettes are given to the winners in riding competitions. In the US, blue signifies first place, red second, yellow third, and green fourth. Tricolor rosettes are given for championships.

Tricolor rosette

You must wear a hard hat at all times when riding

Visiting a horse show
You can see horses in sports such as show jumping, dressage, and driving events at horse shows. They range from a riding club's gymkhana or local steeplechase, to county and international shows.

Going riding
The American Riding Instructors Association has a list of approved instructors and schools and can help you find a local school. The school will provide you with a hard hat, but it is a good idea to wear long pants and a long-sleeved shirt to protect your skin if you fall off.

Knocking down this pole would incur four faults

Jodhpurs are more comfortable for riding than ordinary pants

Equipment
After a few lessons, if you decide you want to continue riding, you can invest in riding clothes. The first and most important things to buy are a hard hat and riding gloves.

USEFUL WEBSITES

- For information on programs at local clubs throughout the United States
www.ponyclub.org
- Learn about the evolution of horses and how they changed the world
www.pbs.org/wnet/nature/horses-introduction
- See beautiful horses of every breed here
www.horsechannel.com
- For horse information, stories, puzzles, trivia, and photos
www.horsefun.org
- Find information on competitions and USEA events
www.eventingusa.com

Pony club silver trophy

Two Camargue horses

All Camargue horses are the same gray color. Younger animals may be darker, but their coats lighten with age.

Seeing horses in the wild

Several breeds of pony live wild in the US. Two herds make their home on the island of Assateague. The herds, separated by a fence a the Maryland-Virginia state line, wander the beaches, roads, and trails on the island. The small shaggy horses are not used to people.

Fly fringes over the horse's ears help cut out distracting sounds

Shire horses pulling a plow

Seeing different breeds of horse

Your local county or state show is a good place to see horses. Larger shows will provide more variety—Stadium Jumping Inc. and Horse Shows in the Sun both give information on where to see shows featuring different breeds.

PLACES TO VISIT

NATIONAL MUSEUM OF RACING AND HALL OF FAME, SARATOGA SPRINGS, NY

The museum and hall of fame is across from historic Saratoga Race Course, the oldest operating track in the US. The museum houses an equine art collection, trophies, and racing memorabilia.

THE HUBBARD MUSEUM OF THE AMERICAN WEST, RUDOSO, NM

The museum contains thousands of horse-related items, including carriages, wagons, horse-drawn vehicles, and artifacts of horse racing's most legendary horses. There are classes and special events for children and families.

NATIONAL COWBOY AND WESTERN HERITAGE MUSEUM, OKLAHOMA CITY, OK

Exhibits include the American Cowboy Gallery and the American Rodeo Gallery. Events include the Chuck Wagon Gathering in May and the National Children's Cowboy Festival.

THE CHINCOTEAGUE VOLUNTEER FIREMAN'S CARNIVAL, CHINCOTEAGUE, VA

The main event at the internationally recognized Pony Penning and Auction is watching Assateague Island's wild horses swim across the Assateague Channel to the mainland at low tide. The event, each July, attracts thousands of people.

THE KENTUCKY HORSE PARK, LEXINGTON, KY

A working horse farm with around 50 breeds of horse. It includes two museums, parade of breeds, and demonstrations of farrier's skills.

THE KENTUCKY DERBY MUSEUM, LOUISVILLE, KY

High-tech, hands-on displays and interactive video exhibits bring the Kentucky Derby to life at this museum.

A racehorse being exercised on Newmarket Heath

Glossary

African wild ass

ARAB
One of the oldest breeds of horse. Arab horses originate from the Arabian peninsula, where they were bred by the Bedouin people about 3,000 years ago.

ASS
A member of the horse family. There are three types of ass—African wild ass (*Equus africanus*), and Asian wild asses (*Equus hemionus* and *Equus kiang*).

BARB
One of the earliest horse breeds. The Barb comes from North Africa, and is the mount of the Berber people.

BIT
The part of a bridle that fits in the horse's mouth. Different styles of bit include the snaffle, curb, and pelham.

BLAZE
A white marking on a horse's head.

BRAND
A mark burned on to a horse's skin to show its breed or who owns it.

BRIDLE
The headgear used to control a horse.

BRUMBY
A type of feral horse found in Australia.

BURRO
A type of feral donkey first introduced to the desert of North America by the Spaniards in the 1500s.

Bridle

CANTER
A gait in which the horse's feet hit the ground in three beats.

CHIVALRY
The qualities expected of a knight in the Middle Ages, such as courage, honor, and courtesy.

COLDBLOODS
The name given to an ancient group of horses from northern Europe. Modern-day heavy or draft horses, such as the Shire Horse, Percheron, and Jutland, are descended from these horses.

COLT
A male horse that is less than four years old and has been castrated.

CROSSBRED
An animal produced by breeding between two horse family members, or between two horse breeds.

CRUSADES
Military expeditions by European knights in the Middle Ages to capture the Holy Land (modern-day Israel).

DOMESTICATION
Donkeys were domesticated in western Asia and Egypt about 6,000 years ago, followed by horse domestication in Asia and eastern Europe.

DONKEY
A domesticated ass, descended from the African wild ass (*Equus africanus*).

DRAFT HORSE
A horse used to pull heavy loads and work the land, rather than for riding.

DRESSAGE
A competition in which a rider shows a horse's skills in obedience.

EQUIDS
Members of the horse family of mammals, which includes domestic horses, wild asses, and zebras.

EQUITATION
The art of horse riding.

FERAL
An animal that is descended from domesticated ancestors, but has returned to live in the wild.

FETLOCK
Part of a horse's leg that sticks out just above and behind the hoof. A tuft of hair often grows at the fetlock.

FILLY
A female horse under four years old.

FLAT RACING
Racing horses on a track with no jumps or other obstacles.

FORELOCK
The tuft of hair on a horse's forehead.

GALLOP
A fast gait in which the horse's feet hit the ground in four beats, and then all four feet briefly come off the ground.

GAUCHO
A cowboy from the South American pampas. Gauchos use horses to round up their cattle.

HAND
A unit of measurement used to work out a horse's height. One hand is 4 in (10.16 cm). Height is measured from the ground to the top of its shoulders.

HARNESS
The equipment of straps and fittings by which a horse is fastened to a cart or other vehicle and controlled.

Dressage

Mane

HINNY
An animal produced by interbreeding a horse and a donkey. A hinny has a horse father and a donkey mother.

HOOF
The horny part of a horse's foot.

HORSEPOWER
A unit of power used to measure an engine's pulling power. One horsepower is the power required to lift a weight of 165 lb (75 kg) a distance of 39 in (1 m) in one second and is equal to 746 watts.

HOTBLOODS
The Thoroughbred and eastern breeds of horse, like the Arab and Barb. The name comes from the hot

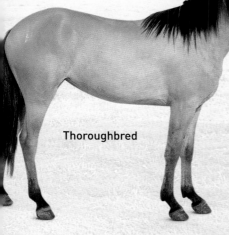

Thoroughbred

countries of North Africa and Arabia in which these breeds originated.

JENNY
A female donkey.

JOUST
A combat between two knights in the Middle Ages to practice fighting skills.

LIGAMENT
A band of fibrous tissue that links two bones and allows a joint to move freely.

MANE
The long hair that grows from the back of a horse's neck.

MARE
A female horse aged four or more.

MULE
An animal produced by breeding between a horse and a donkey. A mule has a donkey father and horse mother.

MUSTANG
A feral horse in North America.

MUZZLE
A horse's nose and mouth area.

ONAGER
Another name for the Asian wild ass (*Equus hemionus*).

PACE
A two-beat gait in which two legs on the same side of the horse move forward.

PACK ANIMAL
An animal used to carry loads.

PIEBALD
A horse's coat with large, irregular patches of black and white.

POINTS
External parts of a horse, such as its poll, pastern, withers, and fetlock.

PONY
A horse less than 14.2 hands (58 in/147 cm) high.

PRZEWALSKI'S HORSE
The only surviving wild horse. This horse became extinct in Mongolia in the 1960s, but is being reintroduced from herds bred in captivity.

RODEO
A competition in which North American cowboys show off their skills at horseriding and handling cattle.

SHOWJUMPING
A sport in which horses are ridden around a course, featuring fences to jump.

SIDESADDLE
A position in which both the rider's legs are on the left side of the saddle.

SKEWBALD
A horse coat, with large white patches on another coat color.

SPUR
A U-shaped device fitted to a rider's boot heels, used to urge a horse forward.

STALLION
A male horse who is four or more years old, and has not been castrated.

STEEPLECHASE
A race over fences and open ditches.

A South American spur

STIRRUPS
Two leather loops suspended from a horse's saddle with metal footrests to support the rider's feet.

STRIPE
A long, white stripe on a horse's head.

THOROUGHBRED
A horse whose ancestry can be traced back to one of three famous stallions.

TROT
A gait in which the horse's feet hit the ground in two beats.

WALK
A four-time gait in which each of the horse's legs hits the ground separately.

WARMBLOODS
Breeds of horse that are crosses between hotbloods and coldbloods.

WITHERS
The top of a horse's shoulders.

ZEBRA
A member of the horse family, found in Africa, that has a coat patterned with black and white stripes.

Przewalski's horses

Index

Acknowledgments

Dorling Kindersley wish to thank:
Alan Hills, Dave Gowers, Christi Graham, Sandra Marshall, Nick Nicholls, and Barbara Winters of the British Museum, and Colin Keates of the Natural History Museum for additional special photography; Clubb Chipperfield Limited, Foxhill Stables & Carriage Repository, Suzanne Gill, Wanda Lee Jones of the Welshpool Andalusian Stud, Marwell Zoological Park, the National Shire Horse Centre, Harry Perkins, and the Whitbread Hop Farm for lending animals and vehicles for photography; The Household Cavalry for providing the rider and the drum horse, and The Knights of Arkley for the jousting sequence; The Berrriewood Stud Farm, Carol Johnson, and Plough Studios for their help in providing arenas and studios for photography; Dr Alan Gentry of the Natural History Museum, Christopher Gravett of the Royal Armories (HM Tower of London), and Rowena Loverance of the British Museum for their research help; Kim Bryan for editorial consultancy; Céline Carez, Hannah Conduct, Liz Sephton, Christian Sévigny, Helena Spiteri and Cheryl Telfer for editorial and design assistance; Jane Parker for the index; Stewart J Wild for

proof-reading; David Ekholm–JAlbum, Sunita Gahir, Susan Reuben, Susan St Louis, Lisa Stock, and Bulent Yusuf for the clipart; Neville Graham, Sue Nicholson, and Susan St Louis for the wallchart; Andrea Mills for text editing and Hazel Beynon for proofreading.

The publisher would like to thank the following for their kind permission to reproduce their images:

Picture credits:
t=top, b=bottom, c=center, l=left, r=right

Aerofilms: 21tl.
Allsport: 58tr Vandystadt; 59br Ben Radford.
American Museum of Natural History: 8cl, 9br.
Ardea: 14clt, 14cl, 16c, 17cr Jean-Paul Ferreo, 17bl Joanna van Grusen.
Barnaby's Picture Library: 43cr; 45bl.
Bridgeman Art Library: 41tl Archiv fur Kunst & Geschichte, Berlin; 34bl Biblioteca Nacional, Madrid; 24tr, 51cbr, 60c British Library; 49tl Guildhall Library; 39cb Harrogate Museums and Art Galleries; 35t, 41tl, 56tl, 59tc Private

Collection; 57ct Smithsonian Institution, Washington, DC; 32bl Musée Condée, Chantilly; 58tl (detail) Musée d'Orsay, Paris; 60tr (detail) Louvre, Paris.
Trustees of the British Museum: 4ctr, 7br, 16tl, 17br, 22tl, 22cl, 22br, 23tr, 26c, 28c, 33tr, 33bl, 46bl.
Bruce Coleman Ltd: 12bl C Hughes; 18b J. & D. Bartlett; 39tl C. Henneghien.
Mike Dent: 23tl, 27tl, 46ctl, 50tr, 54cl, 63tr.
Dorling Kindersley: 37tr Dave King (by courtesy of the National Motor Museum, Beaulieu); 27tr, 36tl, 38 (all except 38br), 40bl, 41 (all except 41 tl, 41 br), 50c, 50–51 b, 51tr, 51c, 51cr, 56bl, 63bc Bob Langrish.
Mary Evans Picture Library: 23bl, 32tr. Robert Harding Picture Libary: 21cr, 24cb, 48tr, 51be, 56cr.
Alan Hills: 20bl.
Hirmer: 33tl.
Michael Holford: 31tc, 44tl, 47tc, 59bl, 60bl.
Hulton Picture Collection: 53b, 63bl. Kentucky Horse Park, U.S.A 67cb. Frank Lane Picture Agency: 12br. Bob Langrish: 13c, 20bl, 37tl, 40br, 41br, 54cr, 56l, 57t, 58bc. 59tl, 59tr, 61tl, 61tc, 65br, 66–67.
Jim Lockwood, Courage Shire Horse Centre, Berks. 67bl.

The Mansell Collection: 42bl. Peter Munt, Ascot Driving Stables, Berks 67tr. Prince D'elle, Haras National De Saint Lo, France, 66bc.Natural History Photographic Agency: 14br Patrick Fagot; 21br E. Hanumantha Rao; 36bl, 60cl A.N.T. Peter Newark's Western Americana: 34tr, 34cl, 43tl, 48cb, 55tl, 57cb, 57bl, 62t.
Only Horses: 37c, 62bl.
Oxford Scientific Films: 17tc/Anup Shah/Okapia.
Planet Earth: 19br Nick Greaves.
Pegas of Kilverstone, Lady Fisher, Kilverstone Wildlife Park, Norfolk. 65br;
Spin way Bright Morning, Miss S. Hodgkins, Spinway Stud, Oxon 66tr.
Ann Ronan Picture Library: 6tr.
The Board of Trustees of Royal Armories: 2c, 43cl, 45tc, 45cr.
Whitbread Brewery: 13cr.
Zefa: 12tr, 13tr, 24clt, 24bl, 25cr, 35br, 36cl, 46cb, 52cl, 52br.

Illustrations: John Woodcock

All other images © Dorling Kindersley

For further information see:
www.dkimages.com